iLEAD™ Tools

PEOPLE
LEADERSHIP

Edited by Stuart Duff

Published by:
Pearn Kandola Publishing
9400 Garsington Road
Oxford Business Park
Oxford
OX4 2HN

ISBN: 978-0-9562318-4-0

British Library Cataloguing in Publication Data
A Catalogue record for this book is available from the British Library.

Printed in Great Britain by Ashford, Hampshire

● CONTENTS

Meaning 117

List of contributors (alphabetical)

Jon Atkins	Emma Kirk	Sally Rendall
Rob Barkworth	Stephan Lucks	Ceri Roderick
Sean Boyle	Joe MacAree	Paul Rose
Clíona Diggins	Ken McKenzie	Maraliese Spies
Polly Howard-De La Mare	James Meachin	Clair Thurgood
Holly Jones	Padraig Neary	Emma Trenier
Simi Jutla	Neil O'Brien	Maggie Van Den Heuval
Laura Haycock	Paula Philips	Louise Weston

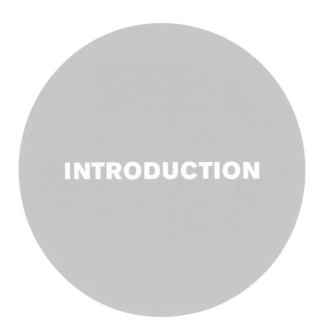

INTRODUCTION

This book is one of three in a series of leadership books based on the coaching experiences of Pearn Kandola Business Psychologists. Any manager aspiring to lead others will have a compelling interest in their own personal development. As coaches and experts in leadership skills, we have created iLEAD™, a series of three unique books based on the most important elements of business psychology.

Over the past thirty years we have coached leaders from hundreds of different organisations across all sectors. Using a combination of our own models and the best emerging research, we have helped those leaders to engage in change and further their development.

Now, for the first time, we have captured these models in three distinct books, one focused on people leadership, one on task leadership and one on thought leadership. Each book offers a chance for any manager to use some basic but essential psychology to help to improve and develop your approach.

A Model of Leadership

Each iLEAD™ tool provides immediate insights and new ways of thinking about management and leadership challenges. There are also a range of interactive exercises to develop new understanding and practise new skills.

The iLEAD™ tools are based on our own strategic model of leadership, known as the Leadership Radar™. The model recognises that there are three core areas of leadership: People, Task and Thought. We use the analogy of a radar because leaders need to have an awareness of these three core areas to fulfil their role and be aware of where and how they use their time across each of the three areas.

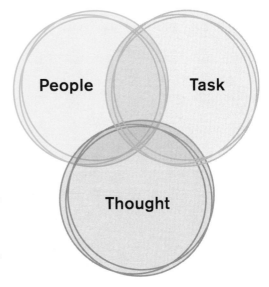

People Leadership

The people leader inspires others towards achievement of ambitious goals through a combination of communication, influencing and engagement skills. They are openly passionate about what they aim to achieve, yet caring and considerate in the way that they approach others. They know that people are their most valuable resource and will do their utmost to secure and retain the commitment of their teams.

Task Leadership

The task leader drives others towards achievement of ambitious goals through a combination of determination, resilience and clarity of focus. They take ultimate responsibility for the quality and delivery of results, and are highly skilled in the way that they delegate tasks and ensure that others are aware of the priority targets. They optimise performance and realise the full talents of the people around them in achieving results.

Thought Leadership

The thought leader constantly looks to new opportunities and the future. They quickly evaluate complex and ambiguous situations and are ready to analyse and challenge tough decisions. The thought leader initiates changes and improvements, and is imaginative and open to taking entrepreneurial risk.

Leadership Styles

There is clearly more than one way to lead. Leadership draws on a diversity of talent and resources, and the most effective leaders understand how to make the most of the situations and people around them. The keys to successful leadership therefore are self-awareness and the capacity to change. While we may at times understand the attributes of leadership, we can often struggle to demonstrate these at the times when they are most needed.

Our aim, therefore, is always to equip leaders with the skills they need, and more importantly to provide them with the motivation and desire to lead. The iLEAD™ tools address both of these challenges.

We hope you not only enjoy reading the tools, but also find ways to make immediate and practical use of them in your own approach to leadership.

MOBILISING

HOW TO MOTIVATE OTHERS

Understand how to get the best from others in your working environment.

⬤ ISN'T IT INTERESTING?

Love 'em or hate 'em, rats are smart, and they've been explaining a thing or two to us. They've been at the leading edge of psychological research into what motivates us and how, which is helpful. Thanks, mates.

How do we motivate others?

People are motivated by all kinds of things. At the most basic level, we're driven by simple needs, as we illustrate below. Once these needs are satisfied, what motivates or gives us purpose, varies with each of us.

Trick or treat

In a series of revealing and insightful studies into motivation and survival back in the 1970s, researchers managed to 'teach' rats to ring bells, pull levers and escape from a complex maze.[1] How? By tapping into the most basic of animal and human needs, providing food as an immediate and positive reward for action.

Rats were put in boxes with a simple lever and a food chute. Each rat would typically run around the box, scratching, climbing and exploring until eventually it accidentally pulled on the lever. This caused a pellet of food to be released down the chute. Initially, the rats made no association between lever and food, but after a few consecutive taps of the lever, they recognised the connection, pressing the lever more frequently for food pellets. The researchers then alternated the delivery of the food, sometimes delaying its timing or changing the effort required to get it – in much the same way that work and targets can be adapted!

These experiments are now recognised as critical to our understanding of learning and motivation. They provided new insights into the most basic way our actions can be (and often are) reinforced by positive rewards. Of course, we're not rats, but we share the same basic needs.

This tool can help

Rewarding behaviour is one of our simplest approaches to motivation. It's the one many parents and teachers use to encourage children's learning, and is still the basis of many 'employee reward' schemes. There are, however, other ways to get results. This tool is about how to motivate others and get the best from them in the working environment.

● UNDERSTANDING MOTIVATION

Motivation

Think you lack motivation? Not so — we're all motivated, it's just that it isn't always easy to know exactly what drives you. It's even more of a puzzle, since everyone's different, to work out what motivates others.

So, if managing others involves knowing how to motivate them, what do you need to know to get the best out of people — and yourself?

Motivation — The facts

There are many theories,[2] some of which add more to our understanding than others. Such theories proliferate because motivations differ according to circumstance and from one individual to another. However, we will summarise some of the enormous amount of research undertaken, (much of it's quite hard work to read and doesn't translate easily to practical, daily application) and note the findings which are relevant and most useful to managers, below:

- People have basic and essential needs — food, comfort, security — that they strive to satisfy. Once these are satisfied, they turn to 'higher' needs, like self-growth and personal fulfilment.

- Generally, people compare themselves to those around them in the workplace; they need to feel they are treated fairly (equitably) in relation to colleagues.

- Setting stretching but achievable goals usually motivates people to achieve more than they would without any goals.

- People are often (but not always) motivated by positive rewards and recognition.

- People's motivations are influenced by two factors: satisfaction and dissatisfaction.

- Satisfaction is primarily the result of 'motivator' factors, which enhance satisfaction but don't necessarily do much to counteract dissatisfaction.

- Motivator factors include: status, opportunity for advancement, gaining recognition, responsibility, challenging/stimulating work, sense of personal achievement and personal growth.

- Dissatisfaction is primarily the result of hygiene factors. (See what we mean? — this is nothing to do with people not washing properly, it's a term used by psychologists to mean 'external!') These factors, if absent or inadequate, cause dissatisfaction, but their presence has little effect on long-term satisfaction. Hygiene factors operate independently of those to do with motivation, so an individual can be highly motivated in his work but dissatisfied with the environment in which he does it. 'Hygiene' factors include:
  - Company policy and administration
  - Wages, salaries and other financial remuneration
  - Quality of supervision
  - Quality of interpersonal relations
  - Working conditions
  - Feelings of job security.

- People are also often more motivated by a need to avoid threat than to seek out opportunities – because most of us are more aware of threat than reward. We are, therefore, seemingly more likely to take risks to avoid negative outcomes than to achieve positive ones.

Recent research[3] lists the top 'motivators' at work as:

1. Accomplishing something worthwhile
2. Learning new things
3. Personal development
4. Autonomy

(Interestingly, pay was 12th on the list and chance for promotion 17th.)

Since all this refers to the majority of us, it's worth remembering when setting goals, reviewing salaries, putting a new team together or just trying to encourage and fire people up. It's useful in everyday interactions, too.

The table below gives ideas and tips for motivating other people, devised from the research we outlined above.

Top Motivational Tips

Make an assessment of what motivates your colleagues. Do this by talking to and observing them. Think about the following:

- What do they say is most important to them at work/home?
- What gives them the greatest feeling of achievement and reward?
- What switches them off?
- What do they get most emotional about in discussions?
- What do they most value?

Do or say things that relate to whatever motivates them

- It will help to obtain their 'buy-in'.
- Explain how changes will relate to what they care about.
- Adapt your own behaviour to include things which motivate them.

Use goals/set targets to motivate

- Make sure you know the difference between a challenge and an unachievable goal.
- Set goals for organisational/team requirements but which also give opportunities for personal development, learning and achievement.
- Break down the goal or target to smaller ones to give individuals more opportunity to feel they are achieving and progressing.
- Set regular reviews of progress and celebrate successes. Give help and advice to overcome hurdles and re-focus attention.

Be transparent

- Give as much information as possible to ensure people understand why they might be treated differently from their colleagues in terms of pay and conditions.
  Note: such differences should only ever be based on merit or competence.

Up to here, we have dealt with the most basic principles. Next we'll explore the more obvious differences between people and their corresponding needs and motivators at work...

● MOTIVATION – HOW ARE PEOPLE DIFFERENT?

Think about your team members or colleagues. You can probably describe the most obvious differences in the ways they work. Some may be energised by new ideas and concepts, others by the detail. Some will come alive talking directly to clients and socialising with colleagues, then there'll be those who only light up when it's time to go home! While generalisation is a dangerous thing, it's useful to highlight the most common characteristics of different types, what their 'needs' are and, therefore, what motivates them. See if you can recognise any of your team members or colleagues in the descriptions here:

A Need to Achieve…

What you'll see: Outward drive, competitive behaviour, impatience with themselves and others, intolerance of others' mistakes, always busy.

How to harness it: Set stretching targets, give autonomy for results, set competitions, set clear timescales, avoid ambiguities.

Watch out for: Burn-out, signs of anger, disappointment at failure, over-reactions to negative feedback, doing too much.

A Need to Please…

What you'll see: React positively to feedback, back down quickly in arguments, present their results positively.

How to harness it: Set challenging (but reasonable) goals, make the goals visible to others, make the goals part of a collective team effort, offer praise publicly and regularly.

Watch out for: Individuals becoming too compliant, being easily upset by criticism, putting others ahead of own needs & being over-sensitive to negative feedback.

A Need to Belong…

What you'll see: Highly sociable, eager to talk to others, enjoy team working, adaptable, outwardly friendly and cohesive style, a 'team' person.

How to harness it: Include in team activities, giving people-focused responsibilities, create opportunity to build relationships.

Watch out for: Being easily distracted, difficulty working independently, being over-sensitive to relationship challenges.

A Need for Autonomy…

What you'll see: High independence, desire for freedom, self-management, controlling behaviours, tendency to work outside the rules.

How to harness it: Break tasks into separate chunks, provide management responsibilities, agree overall targets (not every step).

Watch out for: Lack of communication, detachment from teams, over-controlling behaviour.

A Need for Variety...

What you'll see: Interest in new ideas, start-up rather than closure, flexibility, moves easily from one task to another.

How to harness it: Encourage innovation, involvement at the start of projects, provide opportunities for a change of environment and responsibilities.

Watch out for: Signs of boredom, lack of follow-through and closure, putting personal agenda ahead of business agenda, being too flexible with regulations.

A Need for Structure...

What you'll see: Organisation, reliability, predictability, structured work, plenty of planning in meetings and a need for clarity.

How to harness it: Plenty of clarity when planning, build in clear structures for meetings, regularly agree goals and targets, engage in projects that need micro-managing.

Watch out for: Inflexibility, uncertainty when dealing with ambiguity, being overly rule-bound, perfectionism.

A Need to Care...

What you'll see: Considerate behaviours, concern for welfare, questions based on feeling more than fact, empathy, support.

How to harness it: Put into a support role within the team, give 'people responsibilities' to manage.

Watch out for: Avoiding confrontation, over-sensitivity to others' comments, tolerating too many requests for support, lacking a 'task focus'.

A Need for Control...

What you'll see: Highly organised, planful and detailed approach, strong dislike of ambiguity.

How to harness it: Provide opportunities to manage tasks and projects, provide them with team responsibilities, capitalise on personal organisation.

Watch out for: Tension/frustration with ambiguity, poor delegation ('telling' others, rather than influencing them).

● IDENTIFYING MOTIVATORS – A QUESTIONNAIRE

This will help you reflect on your own and/or your colleagues' motivation. It's about what you see in others' behaviour at work. When designing this questionnaire we used research about people behaving in ways that reflect their personal values (what matters to them). Bear this in mind when you look at the results, because like most theory, it's useful but not bomb proof!

It won't take more than about five minutes and you'll have a 'map' of your own and others' 'primary motivators' – you could make copies for however many people you have in mind.

'Motivation Web' instructions

1. Using the right-hand box, tick any of the statements that clearly apply to you/your colleagues.

2. Once you've responded to all statements, add up the number of ticks for each section.

3. Using the Motivation Web(s) mark each score on the appropriate part of the 1-5 scale, treating the innermost mark as a score of 1 and the outermost mark as 5.

4. Finally, join each of the scores together to reveal the high and low motivators around the web.

Section 1: Need to Achieve

1. Works with a strong sense of urgency

2. Is often impatient

3. Enjoys competing with others

4. Sets self demanding targets

5. Shows strong disappointment at failure

Section 2: Need to Please

1. Smoothes over conflicts in the team

2. Cooperative – is often looking to help others

3. Responds quickly to a pat on the back

4. Takes others' comments very much to heart

5. Eager to please/impress others

Section 3: Need to Belong

1. Sociable and talkative

2. Cohesive in teams – pulling people together

3. Adaptable in teams

4. Avoids conflict with colleagues

5. Easily distracted by others

Section 4: Need for Autonomy

1. Often chooses to work independently

2. Manages self – non-reliant on the support of colleagues

3. Makes up own mind – not easily influenced by others

4. Can be distracted

5. Prefers to take control of situations where possible

Section 5: Need for Variety

1. Excited by new ideas
2. Starts new projects but doesn't finish them
3. Easily bored
4. Follows own agenda – expedient
5. Innovative approach

Section 6: Need for Structure

1. Organised
2. Reliable
3. Dislikes ambiguity
4. Plans work well
5. Communicates frequently, clearly and consistently

Section 7: Need to Care

1. Considerate to others' situation
2. Genuine concern for colleagues' welfare
3. Empathetic
4. Supportive
5. Tolerant of others

Section 8: Need for Control

1. Takes control of team activities
2. Sees others' support as interference
3. Does things in own way, regardless of feedback
4. Becomes tense in uncertain situations
5. Finds it difficult to delegate to others

● THE MOTIVATION WEB

Name

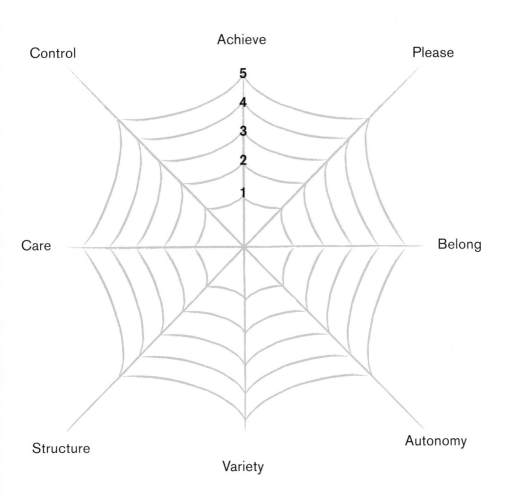

● NEXT STEPS

By now, you should have one (or more) motivation 'webs' on the chart. You can use these to:

1. Identify any 'highs' and 'lows' for yourself and others, and note how these insights could contribute to your own management, team contribution and other work-related subjects.

2. Identify any differences (or consistencies) within your team and consider their implications for the way you work together.

3. Act as a starting point for discussing your performance management targets and the best way to achieve them.

Use the following table, and the information you collected on the previous pages, to consider ways to motivate your team (or whoever else you choose), according to their 'motivators' as identified in their individual webs:

Motivational area	High (4-5)	Low (1-2)
Achieve	● High sense of urgency ● May become frustrated and impatient ● Likes to compete with others ● Sets demanding targets for self and others ● Doesn't take failure well Consider setting them ambitious targets. Encourage them to talk to you before they get frustrated or irritated.	● Low sense of urgency ● May not be focused on high quality levels ● Collaborates with others ● Does not mind making mistakes Ensure you clarify priorities and outline the implications of mistakes. Encourage them to work with others.
Please	● Resolves conflicts in the team ● Will help others to please or impress ● Responds to recognition or acknowledgement ● Takes others' comments very much to heart Take the time to recognise/reward achievements and good work.	● Does not mind upsetting people to ensure tasks completed ● Tolerates criticism and constructive feedback ● Not bothered about making good impressions Gently advise them to take care not to upset others in the team, and give them a more autonomous role in it.
Belong	● Sociable, outgoing and talkative ● Brings people together ● Can modify their behaviour with different people ● Avoids conflict with colleagues Use these people to bring the team together. You could allocate them a co-ordination role in the team. Ensure that they have contact with people.	● Able to work on their own ● Will challenge others in team ● Tends to take their own approach ● Generates ideas and completes task rather than work with people Give these people work to do and involve them in idea generation or strategy. Focus their questioning and challenge constructively.

Motivational area	High (4-5)	Low (1-2)
Autonomy	• Prefers to work independently • Self managing • Makes up own mind • Can appear distracted • Prefers to take control of situations where possible Give them space and autonomy. Monitor to ensure compliance and encourage them to join team activities.	• Works well as part of a team • Reliant on the support of colleagues • Easily influenced by others • Happy to let others take charge Provide them with a central role in the team where they have to work with others. Support them if giving responsibility – but not too much!
Variety	• Excited by new ideas and shows innovation and creativity • Energised when beginning things, less so by completing them! • Can become bored or distracted • May concentrate on own interests Delegate activities to them, keep them busy and involve them in creative tasks and projects.	• May build on existing processes • Prefers routine • Gets upset by change and finds this hard to deal with • Likes to work on one thing at a time Give them clear instructions and limit the number of tasks given at any one time. Clearly explain any change and support them through it.
Structure	• Highly organised and plans work well in advance • Very reliable and works well to deadlines • Dislikes ambiguity and uncertainty • Communicates frequently, clearly and consistently Provide clear structure and frameworks. Give early deadlines to work towards. Conduct regular review sessions.	• Carefree approach, works well with flexible deadlines • Tends to work in bursts of activity • Lacks structure and process • Infrequent or irregular communication Give time and space for work to be completed. Don't be too prescriptive. Expect work to be done but without regular updates!
Care	• Considerate towards others in the team • Shows genuine concern for colleagues' welfare • Empathetic and supportive • High levels of tolerance and patience Give them a role where they can help others learn or develop. Ensure they remain focused on tasks as well as people.	• Not overtly caring towards other team members • Task focused rather than interested in people's lives • May walk over others' feelings to get work completed Give them a more task-focused role. Ensure they consider others before taking action.

Motivational area	High (4-5)	Low (1-2)
Control	• Likes to take control of team activities • Does things in own way, regardless of feedback • Does not like uncertain situations • May find it difficult to delegate to others Provide them with however much responsibility or ownership you're happy to! Clarify the boundaries between their role and those of others.	• Will allow others to lead • Best employed in a supporting role where others take charge • Happy to be told what to do and follow orders • Will delegate work to colleagues if required Give them a supportive role where they can add value and contribute without having to take control. Make their responsibilities clear and offer support.

FURTHER INFORMATION

If you found this tool useful then you are likely to find the following tools both insightful and relevant:

- How to raise energy levels
- How to influence others
- How to develop others
- How to engage others to deliver
- How to use optimism to achieve

REFERENCES

1 Weiner, I. et al. (2003). Handbook of Psychology. John Wiley and Sons.

2 (Maslow's Hierarchy of Needs; McGregor's Theory X/Theory Y; Attribution Theory; Valency Theory; Herzberg's Motivation-Hygiene Theory).

3 Lawler, E. (1994). Motivation in work organizations. San Francisco: Jossey-Bass, Inc.

HOW TO RAISE ENERGY LEVELS

Explore the link between motivation and energy levels and find out how to energise others more effectively through positive thinking.

● ISN'T IT INTERESTING?

Half empty or half full?

Looking at a glass and determining whether it is half full or half empty seems to be the long-standing benchmark for determining whether someone is an optimist or pessimist.

This tool is about raising your energy levels and being able to transfer this energy to the people you work with. Having a positive outlook (seeing the glass half full) is an important part of this because, as the study below shows, optimism can be a key factor in energy levels at work. For more information on optimism see the iLEAD™ tool 'How to use optimism to achieve'.

Why optimism matters

A study by Manju Puri & David Robinson[1] looked into the effects of optimism on behaviour in and out of the workplace. Participants were assessed for optimistic traits using psychometric measures and the pre-existing Survey of Consumer Finance. From this data 3 groups were formed: 'non-optimists', 'moderate-optimists' & 'extreme optimists'.

It was found that there was a higher incidence of behaviour differences in the optimists vs. non-optimists. Optimists are more likely to work harder, expect to retire later, save more and invest in the stock market. The first of these effects is obviously of most interest to this tool, but the others highlight the wide-ranging impact optimism can have.

Furthermore, these various effects indicate increased engagement, at work and outside work, and this can help with raising your energy levels.

This tool can help

There are many situations (whether at work or at home) where that extra bit of energy would be useful. This tool is about how to raise your own energy levels and transmit energy to others. It will help you to explore the link between motivation and energy levels and explain how to energise others more effectively through positive thinking.

17

● TWO FACTOR THEORY OF MOTIVATION

Most of us know what it's like to lack energy, be bored or unmotivated. We don't want to get out of bed and off to work, or we're unenthused by whatever it is we're supposed to be doing. Even so, we all prefer to feel energised, motivated and engaged, knowing it improves our performance. So, we'll explain how to boost your level of energy, and that of those around you, too.

Background

Early research into motivation[2] (Herzberg, 1966) suggested there are two principles associated with motivation or the lack of it. The study investigated when and why people at work felt either positive or negative, and this led to much discussion of 'hygiene and motivation factors'.

Hygiene factors refer to (external) conditions that enhance our experience or which we consider pleasant or satisfying. They don't, in themselves, lead to increased motivation but their absence may de-motivate. For example, feeling underpaid is likely to dissatisfy or de-motivate.

Motivation factors differ from hygiene factors and are necessary to encourage or boost us to perform at significantly higher levels. They're what provide job satisfaction and can spur us to increased effort and performance. So, even though you may now be paid adequately, you're not necessarily motivated. For that, you need to feel you're achieving something.

Dissatisfaction and de-motivation | Employees satisfied but not necessarily motivated | Positive satisfaction and motivation

Hygiene Factors | Motivation Factors

For more information on motivation, see the 'How to motivate others' tool.

Different combinations of hygiene and motivation factors produce different results:

Low Hygiene + Low Motivation = The worst situation of all – de-motivated employees with lots to complain about.

Low Hygiene + High Motivation = Employees are motivated but still complain a lot. It could be that work is interesting or exciting but conditions or salary is poor.

High Hygiene + Low Motivation = Employees don't complain much but aren't really motivated – they may see their job as no more than a means of getting paid.

High Hygiene + High Motivation = The ideal situation. Employees are highly motivated with few complaints.

The kind of hygiene factors which can cause dissatisfaction if employees feel they're inadequate, include:

- Company policy and administration
- Wages, salaries and other financial remuneration
- Quality of supervision
- Quality of interpersonal relations

- Working conditions
- Feelings of job security.

Typical motivation factors necessary to spur effort and productivity include:
- Status
- Opportunity for advancement
- Gaining recognition
- Responsibility
- Challenging/stimulating work
- Sense of personal achievement & personal growth in a job.

Our energy levels, whether at work or in our personal lives, depend on whether the things which motivate us are satisfied. For example, we're much more energised if the tasks and goals we're given at work have meaning or significance for us personally, and this is also true of our relationships and environment.

In the following sections, we're going to discuss what you can do physically to increase your own energy and, then, how to use psychological means of increasing the energy of those around you.

● HAVING THE ENERGY TO ENERGISE OTHERS

There will always be days when you'd rather hide under your desk, let alone have to pull others out from under theirs! Before you can energise them, however, you need to energise yourself. Simply making the decision to take control, being positive and preparing yourself physically is fundamental to energising yourself psychologically.[3]

Straighten up[3]

Your mother was right to tell you to stand up straight! When you slouch, your muscles have to work harder to hold you up, which saps energy. For example, just 15 minutes of reading while slouched or hunched can exhaust the neck and shoulder muscles.

While all processing of our emotions and consciousness occurs in the brain, our body provides key feedback into how we feel and think. For example,[4] smiling uses muscles which then send feedback to the brain making us feel happier. In an extreme example of this, it's been proven that people who have had botox injections to force their face into a more smile-like appearance have elevated moods compared to before their procedure. So think about your muscles as well as your mind when trying to raise your energy levels.

To maintain good posture:

- When standing, keep your shoulders and hips lined up, and your head straight.
- When sitting, use a chair with good lower back support and keep your knees a bit higher than your hips.
- Breathe deeply, inhaling as much oxygen as you can, letting your whole torso inflate before exhaling.
- Don't stay in the same position for too long – try to take a one-minute break every 20 minutes, even if you only walk around your desk!

Drink water

It might not be your first choice when you're feeling in need of a pick-me-up, but tiredness is often a result of dehydration. Other drinks may taste great but won't re-hydrate you as quickly or effectively! Your brain is 85% water and its functions rely heavily on a continual supply of it (studies have shown that brain cells can begin to shrink from prolonged dehydration[5]). Research also indicates that a mere 2% drop in body water can trigger short-term memory problems, trouble with basic mathematics and difficulty focusing on a computer screen or printed page.

The average adult should drink about 6-8 glasses a day — more if you're in a hot environment or exercising.

Eat iron-rich foods

Iron helps your red blood cells transport energising oxygen to every cell in your body. Increasing oxygen supplies, especially to your brain, can make you feel more alert as well as improve concentration and focus. Eating iron-rich foods like red meat, fish, poultry, beans and fortified cereals helps your body maintain energy levels throughout the day.

Blink

The average person blinks two-thirds less when looking at a computer screen.[6] Blinking is a reflex which we tend to do less when concentrating or staring. Blinking keeps the surfaces of our eyes moist, dust-free and clean. Dry eyes become increasingly uncomfortable — so we rub them which makes them water, but it's better to remember to blink more while we work at our computers to reduce the strain.

Break a sweat

According to the National Institute of Health,[7] exercise can energise and keep you more alert because your brain releases natural substances called endorphins. These are thought to relieve stress and pain, giving you a feeling of euphoria or invigoration. Exercise also helps to pump blood around your body, into your muscles and vital organs — including your brain. Psychological benefits can include increased mental alertness (increased concentration, comprehension and memory), reduced stress levels, improved self-confidence and better mood.

The next time you feel yourself flagging at work or can't concentrate, get up and walk around for a few minutes at least — it would be even better if you walked outside in the fresh air! At the very least, stretch and flex your arms and legs.

● TIPS FOR ENERGISING YOUR WORKFORCE

Once you've increased your own energy levels you are in the best place to increase enthusiasm amongst your team.[8] Here are a number of tips for you to try:

Support their careers

You may be surprised to learn that the opportunity to learn and develop motivates many of us as much as, or more than, money. You could renew your team's enthusiasm for their work and careers generally, by formally incorporating specific opportunities into their personal development plans. If you do this, make sure the plans are reviewed regularly to ensure goals are being realised and — just as important — to recognise and celebrate successes.

Cheer them on

Acknowledge your team's contributions and give praise where it's due. Be careful, however, not to constantly praise everyone and everything, or you'll have the opposite effect and people will doubt your sincerity.

Show them you care

Make time for and express personal interest in individuals – without seeming intrusive – even if just a friendly enquiry about their weekend. Ask for opinions about work, working methods and general morale to demonstrate that you value their views.

Make yourself available

Make yourself available and visible so that people regard you as part of the team and willing to help. It will reassure them and may give you additional insight about their daily concerns, or enable you to make more appropriate decisions concerning the whole team.

● ENERGISING OTHERS – ENERGISER OF THE WEEK

Energiser of the week![9]

The purpose of this exercise is to boost the team's energy and productivity with a new strategy and incentive, each week. Making your team responsible for choosing its own weekly incentive will help gain commitment and encourage a feeling of self determination and motivation. This is a great way to build the all-important 'team spirit', too!

It also allows people to contribute different ideas each week – and the variety will stimulate interest, imagination and – most important – fun! If possible, provide a small budget, of say £10-£20 for an energising activity for the workforce.

What to do

Give the 'energiser' as much freedom as possible and make sure they clearly define the result they expect from their idea. They may wish to reduce stress in the team, improve communication or achieve particular targets, and incentives might include a lunchtime video or picnic, changing the office decor in some way as well as the ubiquitous bottles of wine or boxes of chocolates.

The 'energiser of the week' will need to consider team members' interests and motivations when choosing strategies. For example, if the company in question was a video production company, and the team consisted of keen actors, then on a good weather day, the team could go outside and act out some of the videos they'd been working on.

Then…

When every team member has had the opportunity to be 'energiser of the week' get everyone to choose which idea they found most motivating or which worked best by voting 1-3 for each idea – and the winner gets to plan a bigger-scale energiser.

Some ideas to raise morale and get you started

- **Get out of the office** If you work in an office with nice outdoor surroundings, and it's good weather, maybe take an informal meeting outside!

- **Lighten up your emails** If someone has good news or comes up with a good joke, and it's appropriate to share it, feel free to let others join in the fun!

- **Make the most of your office** If you have a communal area, try to make it more appealing by providing newspapers, fruit or games in order to provide a relaxing and pleasant area in the office for those difficult days.

- **It doesn't all have to be hard work!** Introducing a fun non-work activity such as an indoor sport or video games can provide a welcome break from normal work.

- **Play with the dress code** If office regulations allow, hold a themed-dress day for charity, or a regular day for informal wear.

● POSITIVE THINKING EXERCISE

Three Blessings and Sweet Dreams[10]

This exercise is designed to instil a more positive attitude and greater awareness of what's 'good', rather than 'bad'.

Many of us seem predisposed, or 'hard wired' to analyse our own and others' mistakes and failures, rather than celebrate the positives. While this may help us learn and improve it can just as easily be counterproductive, through increasing anxiety, inhibiting creativity and generally undermining our enjoyment of life.

However, with a little effort and practice, we can recalibrate our attitude. Thoughts tend to build on and from each other. There could be much in your day that's 'good', but if you fixate on the few elements which displease you, you'll soon convince yourself that it's all bad. You can just as easily persuade yourself into a positive 'train of thought' – one thought at a time. It gets easier the more you do it, and it feels a whole lot better than the other thing!

What to do

Write

Every night for the next two weeks, write down 3 things that went well each day. It doesn't matter how insignificant you think these might sound to anyone else. For example: 'My partner picked up my favourite ice cream on his way home' or, much more important: 'My sister gave birth to a healthy baby boy'.

Explain

Next to each item on your list, write a possible reason for it. For example, 'because my husband is really thoughtful sometimes' or 'because I remembered to phone him and ask him to bring it'.

Dream

After completing your list and explanations, select one event you'd like to dream about. Positive dreams are thought to increase general wellbeing and consolidate good memories, so it's worth trying to influence them.

Doing the following will increase your chances of a positive dream:

1. Give the positive event a name, e.g. 'my sister's baby'.
2. Visualise it.
3. As you go to sleep, say the name over and over, visualise it and intend to dream about it.

Be prepared to practise – it may take several attempts before you manage to influence your dreams (it works about 25% of the time).

Then...

Continue to take stock of good events in your life, even if you stop writing them down – it's always good to end the day thinking about something positive!

● SUMMARY

Raising your energy levels can be a profoundly exhilarating experience. Be prepared to put in the effort yourself and you're likely to find it's 'catching' and affects others around you!

● FURTHER INFORMATION

If you found this tool useful then you are likely to find the following tools both insightful and relevant:

- How to motivate others
- How to maintain momentum
- How to cope with setbacks
- How to build resilience
- How to get the most out of yourself.

● REFERENCES

1 Puri, M., & Robinson, D. T. (2007). Optimism and economic choice. **Journal of Financial Economics**, 86(1), 71-99.

2 Herzberg, F. (1966). **Work and the Nature of Man.** Cleveland: World Publishing Co.

3 Moore, P. (2012). **The Posture Doctor: The Art and Science of Healthy Posture.** Ecademy Press Limited.

4 Lewis, M. B., & Bowler, P. J. (2009). Botulinum toxin cosmetic therapy correlates with a more positive mood. **Journal of cosmetic dermatology**, 8(1), 24-26.

5 Kavouras, S. (2002). Assessing hydration status. **Current opinion in clinical nutrition and metabolic care,** 5(5), 515-524.

6 Sheedy, J. (2005). **Optometry and Vision Science,** 82, 905-911.

7 www.nlm.nih.gov/medlineplus/exerciseandphysicalfitness.html

8 www.cioupdate.com/career/article.php/3515456.

9 Greenwich, C. (2000). **Energiser of the week: Fun and Gains.** McGraw-Hill Book Co.

10 Seligman, M. (2004). **Authentic Happiness: Using the New Positive Psychology to Realize Your Potential for Lasting Fulfillment.** The Free Press.

HOW TO BE ASSERTIVE

Develop the skills to assert yourself in a range of situations, including coping with criticism; making requests; stating your opinions confidently; and cooperating with others to solve problems.

● ISN'T IT INTERESTING?

Smoke starts to fill the room, what would you do…?

Being assertive

We've all been in circumstances where we've needed to stand up for ourselves, but we've felt the pressure to not do so. Being assertive is all about taking control and being able to put forward your own agenda, even in the face of opposition. Social influence and conformity can be major roadblocks to this (as the study below shows) but knowing this phenomenon and how it works can help you combat it and assert yourself in situations at work.

Where there's smoke…

In a classic psychological study by Latané and Darley,[1] participants were put into a room either a) by themselves, b) with 2 other participants, or c) with 2 stooges who were instructed not to react as the experiment unfolded. Smoke was then pumped into the room.

A. 75% of participants who were alone left to report the smoke

B. 38% of participants who were with 2 other 'naive' participants reported the smoke

C. Only 10% of participants who were with the stooges reported the smoke.

It can be difficult to be assertive and take the lead, even where there may be danger present. One of the conclusions of this study was that togetherness may have reduced the feeling of danger. However, the reluctance to stand out from the crowd may have actually raised the true level of danger.

This tool can help

There are many situations where it is useful and important to assert yourself. This tool is about how to be assertive and will help you to assert yourself in a range of situations. These include coping with criticism, making requests, stating your opinions confidently and cooperating with others to solve problems.

PERCEPTIONS AND RIGHTS

Most of us know people with whom it's easy to get our own way and others who are, perhaps, less persuadable. Being assertive at work can help you keep your workload manageable or get the resources you need for a project.

Assertiveness means standing up for your rights without violating those of others.

You may be surprised to learn that your rights include:

- The right to make mistakes
- The right to set your own priorities
- The right to have your own needs considered
- The right to refuse requests
- The right to express yourself
- The right to judge your own behaviour, thoughts and emotions and take responsibility for the consequences.

Obviously other people have the same rights as you, and some will have authority where you do not. Being assertive does not include being aggressive or failing to acknowledge others' rights.

Here are some examples of some common assumptions in the workplace and how they can sometimes clash with your rights while you are at work. They are general examples in order to broaden your thinking on the subject, and as with anything they could be incorrect if taken to extremes.

However, it is important to think about such examples, because there are plenty of instances where we might be passing up a chance to be assertive out of fear of being 'wrong'. The main thing to remember is that there is nothing 'wrong' about being confident and acting within your rights at work.

Common assumptions and your legitimate rights[2]	
People need to take care of themselves.	Anyone has the right to ask for help or support.
Don't complain or be negative.	You're entitled to be honest about the way you feel.
Advice is usually given from experience and for good reasons – you should follow it.	While it is wise to receive advice, you always retain the right to decide whether to act on it or not.
You're just doing your job, don't expect any thanks.	You're entitled to have your contribution and successes acknowledged.
This is what everybody does in the sector, you just need to turn a blind eye.	You always have the right to challenge an action at work that you believe is unethical by raising it through the proper mechanism.
You need to be sociable, otherwise you're just being difficult.	It's your right to choose when or whether to socialise.
You need to be able to justify yourself.	You do not have to justify your feelings and actions to others if you don't want to.
You should always help those around you before you help yourself.	While it definitely helps to support others, this does not have to be at the expense of your own wellbeing.

● SELF ASSERTION EXERCISE

This exercise[3] will help you identify whether you need to improve your skills in certain circumstances or when dealing with particular people. It has three stages to work through – and an activity sheet to reinforce what you learn.

Stage one – Identify levels of assertiveness

You will need to use the table below for this. The top row of the table describes different types of work relationships; for example, 'Peripheral Relationships' (PAs, cleaners, IT support, etc.), or 'Equality Relationships' (includes others doing the same job as you). Additionally, there are 'subordinate' or 'superordinate' relationships which involve workers who are directly reportable to you, or who you are directly reportable to, respectively.

Underneath each heading, there is space for you to put the name of a person you know who fits the descriptions.

Next, work down the actions on the left to assess your levels of assertiveness with each of the specified people. A good way of judging your assertiveness in a given situation is to ask: *'Do I feel comfortable carrying out this activity with this person?'.*

Rate your response on a scale of 1-4 and insert the number into the table.

1. Very uncomfortable   2. Uncomfortable   3. Comfortable   4. Very comfortable

Once it is completed, this table will help you carry out the next stage of the tool, where you will look at some of these activities in more detail by identifying the areas where you feel most uncomfortable being assertive.

Activity	Person			
	Peripheral relationships (porters, office cleaners, jobs unrelated to ours)	Superordinate relationships (individuals we manage or that work under us)	Equality relationships (colleagues or people performing the same job/grade)	Subordinate relationships (people we are directly answerable to, boss)
Giving praise				
Receiving praise				
Expressing emotions				
Making requests (help, favours)				
Maintaining equal conversations				
Standing up for your own rights				
Refusing requests				
Refusing invitations				
Expressing personal opinions				
Expressing annoyance/ displeasure				
Expressing justified anger				

Stage two – Construct assertiveness behaviour hierarchy

The next stage is to construct an 'assertive behaviour hierarchy'. This can be used to develop short- and long-term goals of how to improve your assertiveness skills. Using the people/actions that you identified in your Stage One table, complete the table below.

Personal assertive behaviour hierarchy

By referring to the matrix you generated in table 1, you should be able to highlight some instances where you could be more assertive with different people. Below is a table where you can list some of the most pressing areas for increasing your assertiveness through specific activities with individuals. You can include people or activities which you did not include in table 1 as well. We have provided a hypothetical example to get you started.

	Person	Activity
1	Rob (Line Manager)	Ask for more reasonable deadlines
2		
3		
4		
5		
6		
7		
8		
9		
10		

Stage three – Assertiveness skills

Now you know when and with whom you need to develop your 'assertiveness skills'. Here are some ways to do this:

Use assertive body language
Face the other person, stand or sit straight, don't use dismissive gestures, be sure you have a pleasant, but serious, facial expression, keep your voice calm and soft – neither whine nor let your voice sound abrasive.

Use 'I' statements

Speak from your own perspective rather than passing judgement on someone else. Example: *'I'd like for this meeting to move at a quicker pace.'* instead of *'You always make meetings go really slowly.'* Using your own perspective makes it more likely that it will be taken as an observation rather than a criticism, and will be more likely to be met positively.

Use facts, not judgements

Example: *'Your punctuation needs work and your formatting is inconsistent'* instead of *'This is sloppy work'*. This makes criticisms or comments objective and fair rather than seeming like you may be impulsive or biased.

Make clear, direct, requests

Don't invite the person to say no. Example: *'Will you please...?'* instead of *'Would you mind ...?'* or *'Why don't you ...?'*

● TECHNIQUES FOR DIFFICULT SITUATIONS

Now that you have identified some specific situations where you could be more assertive, it's time to look at some techniques[3] which might aid you.

Broken record

Keep repeating your point, using a moderate and pleasant voice. Don't get drawn into arguing or explaining yourself. This will prevent you being manipulated, baited, or getting sidetracked by irrelevant information.

Example: You've been handed a report which has been hand-written by a colleague, but the writing is illegible, so you have asked them to type it up for you. However, they become irate and repeatedly say they are too busy, even though you need the review in the next hour. Using the 'broken record' technique, say: *'This writing is illegible, I need it to be typed up please.'* Then, no matter what the colleague says, keep repeating that phrase. Trust us, it works!

Fogging

This is a way to deflect negative, manipulative criticism. Instead of offering denials or counter-arguments you only agree with the facts in an argument. This allows you to keep your own discipline as well as neutralising the argument. Fogging is great for avoiding fights and deflecting criticism, so use it when you notice yourself or someone else getting dragged into a potentially hostile situation.

Example:

Colleague: *'There are some basic mistakes in this spreadsheet you made, you musn't be very good at maths.'*

You: *'Oh yes, I see, there are some errors, I forgot to move that cell over.'*

Colleague: *'It's a pretty stupid error to make.'*

You: *'Yes, I guess it is quite a simple error, I've made a note of it now, and that should mean it won't crop up again.'*

Agree with as many facts as you like, but don't allow the negative criticism about your maths skills or otherwise to be bait for starting an argument.

'Content to process' shift

Sometimes, people will not want to enter a discussion on a particular issue, and will try to block your assertiveness by using humour or distraction to move off topic. In this situation, it can often be helpful to then challenge them on this behaviour directly, before then moving on to the issue you are trying to address.

Example: *'You're getting off the point. I'm starting to feel frustrated because I feel you're not listening.'*

Defusing

Letting someone cool down before discussing an issue.

Example: *'I can see that you're upset, and I can even understand part of your reaction. Let's talk about this later.'*

If they try to stay with it, you always have the right to walk away.

Assertive inquiry/stop action

This is similar to the 'content to process shift'. *'Let's hold it for a minute, something isn't working, what just happened? How did we get into this argument?'* This helps identify the real issue when an argument becomes generalised and bigger than the immediate topic.

Examples include:

Chris: *'Can you help me with this statistics problem?'*

Kim: *'No I can't! You know how much I have to do today!'*

Chris: *'Why is it such a problem to take 15 minutes to help me with this? You told me yesterday that you would!'*

Kim: *'I get so tired of you always asking me to do these things right when I'm in the middle of something!'*

Chris: *'Hold on, let's take a break here. How did we get from my stats problem to you being tired of my interruptions?'*

The real problem here is not that Chris asked for help, it's that he chose a bad time to ask. Through the stop action, *'let's take a break here'*, the two people become aware of the real problem.

Summarising

Summarising the situation helps to make sure you understand the other person.

Example: *'So what you're trying to tell me is...'*

Be specific

It's vital to be clear about what you want done. This helps prevent distractions.

Example: *'The thing I really wish is that you'd pick your clothes up off the floor.'*

Aim to communicate assertively – this means you ask for what you want clearly, openly and explain why in a rational, unemotional way.

DEVELOPING ASSERTIVENESS SKILLS – THE LADDER

Try the LADDER mnemonic[4] to further develop your assertiveness skills:

L **Look at your rights and what you want, and understand your feelings about the situation**
The first stage of the process is to look objectively at the problem. Do what you can to cut away the emotion involved. Try to understand why you feel that your rights are being violated, or why you feel something is wrong with the situation.

A **Arrange a meeting to discuss the situation**
By arranging a formal meeting about an issue, you demonstrate its importance to you. You also ensure time is allocated to discussing it. Sometimes, however, it's appropriate to talk about it straight away.

D **Define the problem specifically**
When describing the problem, keep things objective, unemotional and accurate. Provide supporting information or evidence if appropriate. By talking about any underlying issues you allow the other person to give you additional information which may resolve the situation or alter your own perception of it.

D **Describe your feelings so that the other person fully understands how you feel about the situation**
Once you have explained the facts of the situation, explain how you feel about it in a way that stresses how important it is for you, but without apportioning blame.

E **Express what you want clearly and concisely**
Say precisely what you want to happen. Keep your message short, direct and unambiguous. Be polite – but don't allow this to confuse your message.

R **Reinforce your message to the other person**
Explain the benefits of what you want – how it will improve the situation. Be careful, however, about expressing the negative consequences of not getting what you want. Sometimes this needs to be spelled out but if you make it sound like a threat it could damage a working relationship.

Key take away:

By using an assertive approach, you avoid both the weakness of passivity and the damage that can result from excessive aggression. Assertive approaches promote clear communication and, because all relevant facts and emotions are considered, are more likely to bring about a successful resolution of the situation.

● FURTHER INFORMATION

If you found this tool useful then you are likely to find the following tools both insightful and relevant:

- How to be innovative
- How to think about problems laterally
- How to raise energy levels
- How to motivate others
- How to influence others
- How to communicate your vision.

● REFERENCES

1 Latané, B. & Darley, J. (1970). **The unresponsive bystander: Why doesn't he help?** New Jersey: Prentice-Hall, Inc.

2 Davis, M. & Eshelman, E. (2008). **The Stress & Relaxation Workbook.** New Harbinger Publications, Oakland, CA.

3 Galassi, M. & Galassi J. (1977). **Assert Yourself.** Human Science Press.

4 Smith, M. J. (1985). **When I say no, I feel guilty.** Bantam.

HOW TO INFLUENCE OTHERS

Develop and utilise a range of different styles to persuade and influence your colleagues in the workplace.

● ISN'T IT INTERESTING?

How easily influenced are you?

Use your influence

Most of us would consider ourselves to be reasonably shrewd in decision-making, and not easily coerced into doing something against our will. Much of the research[1] into obedience and authority has shown that we are susceptible to powerful influence from respected figures. This is clearly shown by the classic experiment (outlined below) by Stanley Milgram in the 1960s which has been successfully recreated in modern studies.[2]

A shocking experiment[3]

Unwitting participants were brought into a laboratory setting and told they were taking part in a study aimed to enhance memory by using electric shocks as part of a learning task. They were instructed to question a fellow participant (who was behind a screen) and, upon an incorrect answer, to deliver an electric shock. With each incorrect answer, participants were told to increase the voltage – ranging from 'Slight Shock' to 'DANGER: XXX'. What the participant didn't know was that the person receiving the shocks was actually an actor and the shocks delivered were not real.

Most shocking of all was that the participants, despite believing they were delivering the shocks, continued to question the actor and deliver the shocks. In total, 65% of participants went as far as delivering the 'XXX' shocks when encouraged to do so, even after the actor had complained of heart difficulty and had stopped responding to the questions. The person overseeing the experiment and issuing instructions was wearing a white coat – a clear symbol of authority at that time. Interestingly, in a replication of the study, the location was changed and the scientist was dressed in civilian clothing, without the white coat. These differences saw obedience levels drop significantly, with only 48% of participants willing to deliver the apparently lethal shocks.

This tool can help

This study and subsequent similar studies demonstrate the impact that social influence can have on people. Despite holding independent and rational views, many people feel obliged to be obedient when instructed by an authority figure. Although this type of influence can be used in a negative way, it can also be used positively to achieve business growth. This tool is about how to influence others in a genuine and positive way. It will help you to develop and utilise a range of different styles to persuade and influence your colleagues in the workplace.

● INFLUENCING PEOPLE WITHOUT MAKING ENEMIES

There are mixed feelings about the subject of influence, as well as some confusion. When we describe someone as 'influential' we do so in ways that suggest respect, admiration, even deference – it's a quality to which we seem to aspire. At the same time, however, we're disparaging or suspicious when we recognise attempts to influence us – by politicians, advertisers, friends and sometimes even family. So, is it something we'd all like to be able to do – but only if no one realises we're doing it?

We weren't always so coy. There's a whole industry of self-help books advising parents on how to withstand the ruthless influencing skills of babies and young children. You might remember some of your own tactics which you probably wish you could use in the office, right now: refusal to cooperate, blackmail, bargaining, refusing to give up or in and, when all else fails, yelling.

So, we're all about influencing and being influenced, it's just that as adults we behave more artfully. We've finessed our earlier tactics to work better on peers and superiors using reasoned resistance, negotiation and more respectable forms of perseverance and tenacity.

You need a strategy which will work best for you, according to your personality, but there are some essentials to remember whichever way you go about it.

Remember the following when trying to influence:

- Rapport is essential. Developing a sense of likeability and trust with the person you're trying to influence will only put you in a better position. To learn how to do this, have a read through the iLEAD™ tool 'How to develop rapport'.

- Listen to other people's points of view and try to put yourself in their shoes. It's a great advantage to understand and be able to empathise with someone else's situation, motives and needs if you're going to try and persuade them towards an alternative.

- Identify any common goals, for example 'We all need to get this task completed in 3 weeks.' And also any common points of view or ideas.

- Present your ideas as a suggestion, rather than a proposal. This way, people are more likely to build on your idea, or see it as being flexible, which is positive.

- Make sure you have people's full attention.

- Emphasise why your suggestion is important (particularly where it links to common goals you have already identified), for example 'What does everyone think about splitting the team into two task groups? I think this is important, because we need to complete the task in just 3 weeks.'

INFLUENCING STRATEGIES

Consider the following 'Influencing Strategies' and think how they could be used to acheive greater influence.

Influencing Strategies[4]		
Influence Strategy	Definition	This works when...
Reason	Utilising your logic, information and deducing abilities to justify the request for an action. Providing the evidence for a request allows people to absorb the facts of your viewpoint into their own.	• You have a high level of experience in the matter. • The decision is very fact based.
Assertion	By using direct and forceful requests for an action to be taken, your confidence and motivation in the desired course of action is shown. See the iLEAD™ tool 'How to be assertive'.	• You are experienced at influencing others. • It is a strategic decision, where there is room for debate.
Exchange	This approach involves an exchange of benefits, cooperation and compromise to reach a goal. This makes the request seem mutually beneficial, encouraging the participation of others.	• The views of others need to be accommodated. • You need to maintain a network of relationships to carry out the action.
Courting Favour	This involves being friendly and/or positive to the person you wish to influence. Those who consider you a friend/friendly are far more likely to assist you. See the iLEAD™ tool 'How to develop rapport'.	• You need to build a lasting influence. • There are personal factors involved in potential success.
Coercion	This strategy influences using the threat or application of scolding or punitive actions. This works by discouraging people from not following your plans and activities.	• You are not concerned about the feelings of others. • You have a high level of authority.
Partnership	This involves garnering support from several levels of an organisation in order to get a multi-level consensus. This is likely to increase a feeling of unity and participation in an action.	• Wide participation in a project is needed. • You have a wide network available to utilise.

Knowing how, when and where to use each of these strategies is key to successful influencing. Look for appropriate opportunities where you can practise using the ones you least favour, to develop a range of skills you can use in different situations.

What kind of influencer are you now? Is this the most suitable way to influence people who you currently work with? The six examples below form three pairs of styles to predict the kind of influencing behaviours that people will use.[4] When there is a situation that will potentially require influence, people are likely to adopt an influencing style that will land somewhere on one, if not more of the influencing styles. If you think back to some different work situations in your past, can you identify what kind of influencing style you were using? Bear in mind that, depending on the scenario, your influencing style may have changed (for example if you were tasked with managing a new project with a new team).

Influencing Style	Strategies and Behaviours of Style
Bystander	Bystanders are unlikely to use any influencing strategies. They are unlikely to make use of a network of colleagues, instead being restricted to mainly solitary activities. This strategy is most used when the person is in a purely operational role, and has few or no responsibilities outside of their own workload. Additionally they have low access to key resources and low power or expectation to influence others.
Shotgun	'Shotguns' are the opposite of bystanders; they are likely to use every kind of influencing strategy and use them regularly with great abandon. 'Shotguns' are likely to have a workload that requires them to work through a large network of people and be motivated to have a lasting effect on them and their actions. This is often due to their having great responsibility or accountability for their actions and the need to derive resources from many people.
Strategist	Strategists are likely to use the influencing strategies of 'reason', 'assertion' and, less often, 'partnership'. They have a high expectation of being able to influence, mainly due to their previous experience in a similar situation. Additionally, they tend to be very independent, and not be overly concerned with the needs of others, focusing on their own workload.
Opportunist	Opportunists are more prone to using 'courting favour', 'exchange' and 'coercion' than the other 3 strategies. They tend to have a low expectation of the level of influence they are able to have, based on previous experience in a similar situation. They are dependent on others to help and also to be helped in their own work.
Collaborator	Collaborators use 'exchange', 'courting favour', 'reason' and 'partnership' as their most common strategies. They are aware of and act within the needs of others due to the need to maintain cooperative relationships. There is generally little need to maintain and/or improve the behaviour or productivity of others.
Battler	Battlers will generally rely on the use of 'assertion' or 'coercion' in order to influence others. They normally use these strategies because they have a need to drive change in people's behaviour and productivity due to the influencer having a large strategic role. They normally do not have the need to make goodwill gestures or be overly aware of the feelings of others, and this leads to their use of more forceful influencing strategies.

● KNOW YOURSELF, KNOW THEM, ADAPT

Effective communicating and influencing requires a high level of personal awareness and knowing what impact you want to have on others when you're trying to influence them.

Three skills you should focus on are:

- Self-awareness
- Awareness of others
- Flexibility/adaptability

Self-awareness

The effective influencer must be aware of his or her own skills and abilities and have a clear understanding of their preferred style of dealing with others. They should know their own strengths and weaknesses, motivators and de-motivators and sources of power and have a very clear understanding of their role in the influencing process. For example, if you know that you are good at making people feel at ease, be sure to use that strength at the start in order to get the best result.

Awareness of others

As well as being self-aware, an effective influencer will also be very aware of what makes others tick. Typically, they'll observe others' preferred influencing styles, the skills they use in influencing situations, their power bases and in particular what engages and disengages them. Awareness in this area will help you choose the right approach for whoever is involved, while also remaining open to being influenced by others. For example, if you know that someone you are trying to influence tends to be impatient, try to make your influencing style concise and to the point.

Flexibility/adaptability

The ability to change and adapt to suit the situation is vital. The skilled influencer realises that there is no right way of influencing. There are only effective skills which can help you in the process. The success of any influencing interaction is usually down to how the skills have been used in practice. Adaptability and flexibility are the keys. Flexibility to be able to vary your style and approach to suit the particular situation and people involved as well as the ability to assess the situation and people facing you. Make sure that when you are trying to influence you are doing things like keeping notice of body language, to see how receptive the individual is at that particular moment.

● LEADING A FOOD REVOLUTION

This excerpt from Jamie Oliver's Acceptance Speech at the TED Awards 2010 captures some of these key influencing strategies:

TED (Technology, Entertainment and Design) is a global set of conferences formed to disseminate 'ideas worth spreading.'

'Sadly, in the next 18 minutes when I do our chat, four Americans that are alive will be dead from the food that they eat.

My name's Jamie Oliver. I'm 34 years old. I'm from Essex in England and for the last seven years I've worked fairly tirelessly to save lives in my own way. I'm not a doctor; I'm a chef, I don't have expensive equipment or medicine. I use information, education. I profoundly believe that the power of food has a primal place in our homes that binds us to the best bits of life.

We have an awful, awful reality right now. America, you're at the top of your game. This is one of the most unhealthy countries in the world. Can I please just see a raise of hands for how many of you have children in this room today? Please put your hands up...... aunties and uncles as well. Most of you. OK. We, the adults of the last four generations, have blessed our children with the destiny of a shorter lifespan than their parents. Your child will live a life ten years shorter than you because of the landscape of food that we've built around them. Two-thirds of this room, today, in America, are statistically overweight or obese. You lot, you're all right, but we'll get you eventually, don't worry. (Laughter) Right?

The statistics of bad health are clear, very clear. We spend our lives being paranoid about death, murder, homicide, you name it; it's on the front page of every paper...... Fact: Diet-related disease is the biggest killer in the United States, right now, here today. This is a global problem. It's a catastrophe. It's sweeping the world. England is right behind you, as usual. (Laughter) I know they were close, but not that close. We need a revolution. Mexico, Australia, Germany, India, China, all have massive problems of obesity and bad health. Think about smoking. It costs way less than obesity now. Obesity costs you Americans 10 percent of your healthcare bills, 150 billion dollars a year. In 10 years, it's set to double: 300 billion dollars a year. And let's be honest guys, you ain't got that cash. (Laughter) I came here to start a food revolution that I so profoundly believe in. We need it. The time is now. We're in a tipping-point moment....'

Jamie used the following tactics to influence his audience:

1. **Attention** – Jamie starts by grabbing everyone's attention with a strong emotive statement.
2. **Rapport** – his humour and down-to-earth style help him connect with the audience. They listen to what he has to say because they like him.
3. **Empathy** – he appeals to the issues that matter to the audience most.
4. **Common Goals** – he emphasises how we all share the same challenges to encourage a collective spirit.
5. **Importance** – he spells out the cost and significance of the problem.
6. **Reason** – he uses hard data to validate his points.
7. **Assertion** – he passionately urges action now.
8. **Persistence** – this speech comes after a seven-year tireless campaign that continues to this day.

This carefully crafted speech aims to maximise the power of influence by utilising a wide range of tactics that will appeal to a variety of listeners.

Now take the following steps:

1. Spend a few minutes reading this account again and ask yourself what you can learn from it.
2. Think of a time when you tried to persuade others to support your idea, perhaps starting a revolution of your own!
3. Note down what influencing behaviours you demonstrated.
4. How effective were your skills; did it make others change their minds, or even more importantly, change their behaviour?
5. How many people did you get to join your 'Food Revolution' because they understood the consequences of not doing so?
6. What did you learn from that experience, to ensure you get the required outcome next time? What alternative strategies would you use?

● YOUR INFLUENCING STYLE

Use the table below to identify the personal influencing strategy or strategies that work best for you. Use the table of influencing strategies on page 34 to help you prioritise which ones would be most effective for you to use.

Step 1

Read through the influencing strategies to familiarise yourself with them.

Step 2

Re-prioritise them according to your personal approach. Note down your three most preferred styles. While you're doing this, imagine who you're influencing and which strategies have worked well in the past and that you've used most often.

Influence Strategy	Order of Preference	How can I make this strategy work for me?
Empowerment		
Interpersonal Awareness		
Bargaining/Negotiating		
Relationship Building		
Organisational Awareness		
Common Vision		
Impact Management		
Logical Persuasion		
Coercion		

Remember – you may identify a couple of strategies you prefer to use, but also think about which would work best for different people. You may need to adapt your style to have the most influence in different situations and with different people.

● NEXT STEPS

Now you've considered the information in this tool and tried out some of the practical exercises, here's some advice about how to remember and try out what you've learned.

Look for opportunities to practise

Think about the opportunities that you have in your current work, or elsewhere, where you can practise influencing others. When do you have to influence others in your work? Consider the opportunities that you have with different types of people; for example, senior individuals, groups of people, customers, colleagues, your manager, etc.

Observe other people

Look around the organisation at the different influencing styles people use, and make a note of what you like or seems to work well and what you dislike or doesn't work so well. You can then compare your style in the context of the organisational approach and see how you can adapt to be more effective.

Talk to a role model

Is there someone who you know who influences people easily? If so, you could discuss this topic with them. They may give you advice that helps you be more effective.

Write a development plan

Having completed the exercises in this tool an important next step is to consider what you can do to improve. Make learning how to influence people in different ways part of your personal development plan. If you don't have a plan like this you could put one together, using this topic as a starting point. Ensure you give yourself clear objectives and practical things to do that will help you make real progress.

Get feedback on your influencing style

Have you asked other people how effective they think you are at influencing others – what you do well, what's not so good, what you could do better? Even if you have in the past, this may be a good time to get a more up to date assessment. You can ask anyone but try to make sure that it's someone you trust to be honest (but be prepared to have to ask for this). This could be your line manager, mentor, coach or colleagues, customers and friends. You may want more than one view to get different perspectives.

Set a future date to review your progress

Ask people for comments and see if they've noticed any changes. Make a note of any aspect that could still improve.

Some tips to take away

Know your strengths

You will be more confident, comfortable and convincing in your persuasion if you play to your strengths. If you are analytical, use logic and reasoning. If you are empathic, use active listening and attend to the person's feelings. If you are creative and extrovert, look to make an impression.

Know your audience

What strategies will work will depend on your audience as well as your own ability to apply your skills. This means that you need to gain an understanding of their position, their likely concerns, their motivations and their relationship with you. If you can tap into what makes them tick and allay their concerns then you are more than half-way there.

● FURTHER INFORMATION

If you found this tool useful then you are likely to find the following tools both insightful and relevant:

- How to motivate others
- How to raise energy levels
- How to be assertive
- How to communicate effectively
- How to manage your impact
- How to build and maintain trust
- How to gain buy-in and commitment
- How to engage others to deliver.

● REFERENCES

1   Dambrun, M., & Vatiné, E. (2009). Reopening the study of extreme social behaviors: Obedience to authority within an immersive video environment. **European Journal of Social Psychology**, 40(5), 760-773.

2   Nicholson, I. (2011). 'Shocking' Masculinity: Stanley Milgram, 'Obedience to Authority,' and the 'Crisis of Manhood' in Cold War America. **Isis**, 102(2), 238-268.

3   Milgram, S. (1963). Behavioral study of obedience. **Journal of Abnormal and Social Psychology**, 67, 371–378.

4   Manning, T. (2012). The art of successful influence: matching influence strategies and styles to the context. **Industrial and Commercial Training**, 44(1), 26-34.

CONNECTING

HOW TO DEVELOP RAPPORT

Establish a mutual connection with colleagues to gain the best outcomes from your interactions with them.

● ISN'T IT INTERESTING?

When you meet someone for the first time what do you think?

Do you jump to conclusions about people?

Yes? No? Sometimes? We'll bet most would answer: 'No, of course not.' However, we're all constantly bombarded with information with often little time to make anything other than snap judgements. Some researchers even suggest we're 'hard-wired' that way because we needed to think fairly rapidly back when we were hunting and gathering, fighting or fleeing. The challenge in a work environment is to identify when quick decisions are appropriate and, more important, when they aren't.

Good looking, looking good

In one of the most famous social experiments of recent years, Alex Todorov and colleagues ran a study of how snap judgements can affect the ways we behave towards people.[1] The researchers asked participants to look at a number of faces and rate them each for trustworthiness. They found people did this confidently, within milliseconds of looking at a face. When the participants were given more time to look (a few seconds) their judgements still didn't alter. The only thing that changed was people's confidence in their judgement.

What really amazed the researchers was the degree to which participants were willing to make important judgements (trusting others or not) based only on the way people looked. Subsequent studies have found that we make all sorts of generalised judgements about people, based on nothing more than their looks, and that if we see one outstanding positive feature (such as good looks) in a person, we readily make additional, positive assumptions that they're clever, witty and reasonable. This simple, yet very powerful and consistent finding, is known as the halo effect.[2]

This tool can help

The halo effect is one of many different influences that can shape the way we get to know and understand other people. There are a number of techniques that can be adopted to help us develop stronger rapport and avoid making swift but irrational judgements. This tool is about how to develop rapport and will help you understand how to do it successfully.

● THE IMPORTANCE OF RAPPORT

Why do some people seem able to talk to anyone and others just stand about, all buttoned up? Is it that some of us are naturally more gregarious or can you learn how to find and build a rapport with whoever you need to get on with, say, at work?

It's not about instant likes or dislikes or recognising 'your own kind' of person. Building rapport, with anyone, is knowing how to establish a mutual connection, a warmth which may then enable a degree of trust.

Similar to empathy, rapport helps us communicate acceptance or understanding of another. Although it comes more easily to some than others, we're all able to develop rapport, but we may need to know how, particularly in situations where you need something such as support or advice. The three practical exercises to help build rapport in this tool concern body language, verbal communication and how you reveal your personality and credibility to establish common ground.

What are the outcomes?

Building rapport means that you're more likely to gain the best possible outcomes from meetings and interactions with others. In a business environment, the ability to build rapport facilitates telephone calls, face-to-face meetings, presentations and relationships with colleagues and clients.

As a manager, flexing your style to build rapport with the individuals in your team and clients involves taking the lead and making an effort to create a climate that facilitates better performance management, training and delivery.

Building rapport is about creating an emotional environment which allows genuine communication. Then, connections are made, ideas are developed and productive working relationships are formed.

Below we outline a three-factor model of the process of building rapport.

● 3-FACTOR MODEL OF BUILDING RAPPORT

A landmark study on rapport by Albert Mehrabian[3] measured the impact of voice tone and body language on our perceptions of the trustworthiness of other people. The researchers found that when people smiled warmly whilst saying 'I don't like you' the other person was unlikely to believe what they said. Body language overruled the actual meaning of the words. More specifically they found that:

- 55% of the impression you make comes from your behaviour and your body language.
- 38% of the impression you make comes from your tone of voice.
- 7% of the impression you make comes from the actual words you say.

Based on the findings of this study, and our work in coaching, there are three key elements of building rapport – creating common ground, body language and verbal communication.

3-factor model of building rapport

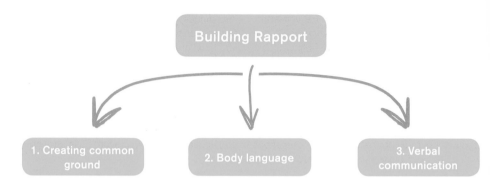

1. Creating common ground

Many factors come into play which affect your ability to build rapport and create common ground. The 'similar to me' bias and the 'halo/horns' effect are two to be aware of:

- The 'similar to me' bias: we're all attracted to types similar to ourselves. The most obvious similarities are gender, race and age, but others include personality and interests. Emphasising your similarity to another, even in small ways, helps build rapport. For example, on finding out that the person you're meeting is interested in sport, mentioning your own, similar interest affirms something in common.

- The 'halo/horns' effect: first impressions are important. They're so important that they can actually determine the course of an entire encounter. If the person you're meeting makes a positive judgement of you in the first minute or so, they are likely to interpret your subsequent actions positively. If they don't view you positively in those first few seconds, they're likely to interpret the very same actions negatively. Paying attention to making a good first impression is vital. This means taking a relaxed, open approach and showing warmth by making eye contact, initiating conversation and projecting a positive attitude.

So building rapport doesn't require you to be somebody you're not. It's about engaging with another person and expressing a real interest in them.

2. Body language

Your body language reinforces the message of your words and can provide a wealth of information about how you're feeling, what you're really thinking and how comfortable you are. Some of the important elements are:

- **Posture and distance** – How close you are to the other person. Too close and you may appear aggressive, too far away and you won't have enough 'personal presence'. This also depends on the posture you adopt.

- **Eyes** – Can you maintain the right level of eye contact? Try to maintain relaxed and friendly eye contact without staring too much or looking uninterested.

- **Mouth** – When we're nervous, we often clench our jaws and tighten our mouths. Try to relax this part of your face and smile to soften your appearance to match your friendly words, or you may send mixed, confusing messages.

- **Gestures** – These include waving your hands, fiddling with things, folding arms and pointing fingers. Open arms and shrugging shoulders may convey passivity or 'giving up', while excessive movements can be distracting.

There are a number of techniques that you can use to create impact through your body language: Here are two of the most powerful.

Mirroring

When you see two people engaged in an intimate conversation you probably notice how they tend to hold themselves in the same kind of body posture, holding their heads in similar ways or making gestures of a similar size. In this context, the two individuals will probably be instinctively mirroring each other. In the same way, you can use 'mirroring' to encourage an easier flow of communication without the other person thinking you're making an extra effort. Matching body language to gain rapport involves adopting a similar posture, giving the same amount of eye contact and matching the speed and general frequency of hand gestures. Don't overdo it, though, or you'll have the opposite effect to what you want!

Mismatching

Mismatching is the opposite of mirroring and can also be useful. Although disengaging, it need not invalidate the other person. It can be used to extricate yourself from a conversation or help bring a discussion to a close. In this situation you may see people increasing distance between themselves and others, or reducing eye contact.

3. Verbal communication

Although the language that we use only accounts for a proportion of our communication, when you match the verbal style of the person you're talking to you can strongly influence rapport. Matching the volume, words, phrases and images used and, to some extent, the beliefs and opinion of the person you're speaking to is known as 'pacing'.

Pacing volume

You can pace the volume of the conversation by speaking more softly to someone with a quiet voice and more loudly to a person with a louder voice. When you match someone in the volume of your voice you indicate you're 'on the same wavelength' and are far less likely to be viewed as threatening. People have a tendency to prefer relating to people they consider similar to themselves and, as a result, feel more comfortable in conversation with them.

Pacing words, phrases and images

The words, phrases and images that people use give us clues about how they perceive the world. Some people tend to think in images (visual), others prefer to discuss a concept to hear how it sounds (auditory) while others need to experience how something feels (kinesthetic).[4] When you pace this aspect of their speech you gain trust by demonstrating that you understand them. You can do this by using words, phrases and images the other person uses, in a way that you're comfortable with.

Pacing beliefs and opinions

Validating some of the things the person you're talking to believes in is affirming and strengthens connection. For example, if you're talking about packaging for a new product you could 'validate' the other person by saying that you thought they'd be interested as you know they are artistic.

Pacing and leading

Once you have paced and matched the state of someone's demeanour you're in a position to move them gently from one state of mind to another with your own body language, gestures and tone of voice. For example, by mirroring the movements of an angry and upset person you acknowledge that their feelings are important. It's then possible to lead them to a 'calmer' state by moderating the tone of your voice and relaxing your posture.[5]

● PACING WORDS, PHRASES AND IMAGES

When you're talking to other people, pay attention to the kind of language they use. Is there a pattern? Do they use words from the descriptions below? Once you've picked up on a theme it's easy to 'pace' the kind of words, phrases and images used.

Language Style	What they may say	Try
Visual	● 'I can see what you mean by that' ● 'I need to be able to picture how this works' ● 'Lets draw a diagram of how these aspects fit together' ● 'To see clearly' or 'To illuminate' ● 'To imagine' or 'To focus' ● 'Unclear' or 'Visualise' ● 'Coloured' or 'To demonstrate'	● Presenting your ideas using pictures and diagrams. ● Sitting back and describing your plan or elements of it like a picture or model. ● Physically demonstrating how something works rather than describing how it works.
Acoustic	● 'Lets talk through that idea so that we can hear how it sounds' ● 'To listen' or 'To hear' ● 'To shout' ● 'To speak' ● 'To call' ● 'To discuss' or 'To chat about'	● Presenting information orally and allowing time for discussion. ● Describing how something works rather than physically demonstrating.
Kinesthetic	● 'I feel like this is going to work' ● 'This seems real to me' ● 'To touch' ● 'To feel' ● 'I feel relaxed about this' ● 'This makes me really tense' ● 'I'm feeling the pressure'	● Describing how things feel to you rather than what you think about them. ● Allowing the other person to try things out before deciding whether they work or not.

● MAKING A GOOD FIRST IMPRESSION

Although you may think you'll know instinctively what kind of first impression you're going to make, it can be helpful to prepare for a meeting with someone you haven't met before by answering the questions below.

● How do you want to come across?

● What do you have in common?

● What are their interests?

This way you will be able to demonstrate both who you are and engage confidently with the other person.

Question	Response
How do you want to come across to the person you are about to meet?	1. 2. 3.
What do you have in common with the person you are about to meet?	1. 2. 3.
What interests you about the person you're about to meet?	1. 2. 3.

● BODY LANGUAGE: PRACTISING MIRRORING

When you demonstrate the same gestures, body position and eye contact as the person you are speaking to, you tend to find that conversation moves more smoothly. Being aware of this means that you can consciously use mirroring as a tool to build and strengthen rapport.

The mirroring exercise

To practise, try sitting with someone you know well and mirroring their body language without telling them what you're doing. You don't need to mirror everything they do, just adopt a similar posture and some of the gestures they use. After a while, change your posture and notice the change to the conversation this causes (see reference 5, Erickson, 2004).

When you try something new you may feel a bit clumsy because it feels unfamiliar, even though you'd probably do it unconsciously with someone close. As with anything, though, practising will help to make it easier and increase your confidence.

● TAKE AWAY MESSAGES

There are three things of particular importance to keep in mind:

1. Building rapport requires some thought and effort, even for those of us who are 'naturally' skilled in this area. Think about the first impression you're planning to make with the person you're about to meet.

2. 'Pacing' the words, phrases, images and, to some extent, the beliefs and opinions of the person you wish to build rapport with enhances communication.

3. 'Mirroring' the body language of the person you're speaking to often happens naturally. Being mindful of using it as a tool will help build rapport more easily with people you don't know very well.

Create and improve relationships

Everyone can learn to build rapport; done well this can have a hugely positive impact on developing and maintaining excellent working relationships.

● FURTHER INFORMATION

If you found this tool useful then you are likely to find the following tools both insightful and relevant:

- How to communicate effectively
- How to manage your impact
- How to build and maintain trust
- How to actively listen.

● REFERENCES

1 Willis, J. & Todorov, A. (2006). First impressions: Making up your mind after a 100-ms exposure to a face. Psychological Science, 17, 592-598.

2 Asch, S. (1946). Forming impressions of personality. Journal of Abnormal and Social Psychology, 41, 258-290.

3 Mehrabian, A. (1981). Silent messages: Implicit communication of emotions and attitudes (2nd ed.). Wadsworth, Belmont, California.

4 Hollman, W. & Kleiner, B. (1997). Establishing rapport: the secret business tool to success. Managing Service Quality, 7, 4, 194-197.

5 Erickson, J. (2004). The Art of Persuasion: How to Influence People and Get What you Want. Hodder Mobius, St Ives.

HOW TO COMMUNICATE EFFECTIVELY

Make your message clear, concise and easily understood, to help you to communicate more successfully with a wider range of people.

● ISN'T IT INTERESTING?

Christmas this year is cancelled…

What type of communication do you respond to?

Consider adverts at Christmas that aim to prevent or reduce how much alcohol people drink before they drive, or appeal for donations to charities. When you see these adverts, do you listen carefully to the message? Or do you swiftly change the channel? Clearly some of these adverts succeed and people's behaviours change, but there are many different ways to communicate messages and these vary depending on the audience's needs.

Shock adverts – do they work?

The bottom line in advertising is that producers want to clearly communicate a message to the audience. This applies to adverts selling products as well as messages to encourage positive behaviour such as health awareness.

A modern study[1] researched the effectiveness of public health adverts in encouraging people to perform health self-examinations. Adverts which induced high, low or no levels of fear had varying levels of success on those who viewed the adverts, but it was not the only dependent factor. What was found to be more important was the level of subjective knowledge about the health issues that the individuals already had. In essence, the level of influence achieved by the advert depended on the person who was watching it.

A similar study[2] showed how other factors, such as gender, can cause different effects. The study involved anti-speeding adverts, and while females believed the adverts would affect themselves more than others, men believed the opposite (it would affect others more than themselves.) As a result, females reported that they were more likely to change their behaviour than men were.

This tool can help

To enable us to communicate effectively, we need to be able to call on a number of different skills. Whilst we all like to think we can communicate well, there can be more to this than we initially think! This tool is about how to communicate effectively and will help you to make your message clear, concise and easily understood. This will help you communicate more successfully to a wider range of people with different backgrounds.

● COMMUNICATING YOUR MESSAGE

If we can't communicate effectively we're unlikely to get what we want, whether that's a train ticket to the right place or persuading a group of people to commit to a new project. In any situation, the first things to think about are who you're talking to and what you want — then, how you're most likely to achieve it.

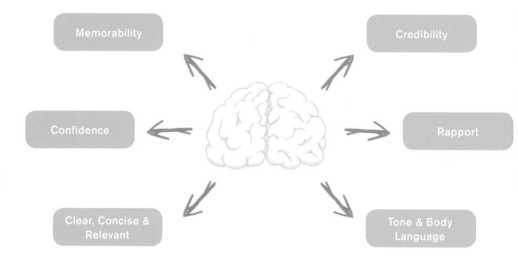

Message

First, the type of message you're trying to get across will determine the way you go about it. You might have several important messages to communicate to an uninterested audience — a group of bored schoolchildren, perhaps — which, instead of listing, you could more effectively incorporate in a story. You also need to remember the result you want; for example, if you're trying to sell something, don't forget to tell people how to place an order!

Audience

You need to tailor your message to the audience and their knowledge of your subject. There's been much research into the effect of the tone we use when communicating, which has produced a theory called 'Transactional Analysis'.[3] The theory is that we have three modes of behaving and communicating: Parent, Child and Adult — and that we tend to respond in ways which take their cue from whichever tone of speech or behaviour is used towards us. So, if someone speaks to us in the authoritative manner of a Parent we'll respond with the typical deference of a Child.

Conversely, if someone opens an interaction in a 'Child' manner, we're more likely to adopt an authoritative response by assuming control or giving instruction. However, when interacting in the workplace we may aim to adopt an 'Adult' tone, which is used for exchanging information, evaluating and decision making. Make sure, therefore, that you don't come across as condescending or critical. 'Adult' interactions are characterised by a confident and inquiring tone, interested and thoughtful body language and an open, evaluative attitude.

Clear, concise and relevant

Use clear, straightforward language and avoid jargon which may confuse or irritate whoever's listening. Make it concise and relevant – digressions can be illustrative or serve to add interest, but expansive detail and irrelevance will frustrate and bore. Avoid repetitions and catchphrases – many of us use a certain phrase habitually ('d'you know what I mean', for example) without realising it!

Rapport

If the audience can relate to you personally, as well as to what you're saying, they'll be more receptive. To learn more about this, see our tool 'How to develop rapport'.

Credibility

Again, if you behave and sound as if you're trustworthy and know what you're talking about, people are more likely to trust you in return, by 'buying-in' to your message. Research reveals that people are more compliant when spoken to by 'authoritative' figures, which includes sounding authoritative, or 'expert' in whatever you're talking about. For example, a recent study[4] showed this is how many religious leaders influence their followers' beliefs.

Confidence

It's not very helpful simply to advise you to be confident if you're anxious or worried about communicating. Think of it like this: If you're confident in your message it will translate to your audience, which is more important than worrying about what people will think about your left profile or whether the stripy socks were a mistake. There's a curious but proven phenomenon called the Pygmalion effect[4] which stems from research into how expectation affects outcome. A recent study showed that when workers in Japan expected a project to go well, they performed better. In other words, if you expect things to go badly, you're increasing that likelihood. Instead, just prepare well, believe in what you're saying and expect it to go well!

Tone and body language

While your message is the most important aspect of your communication, your tone and body language also give subtle messages, so make sure the way you behave doesn't contradict your intention. Maintain an open expression, don't avoid eye contact or give the impression you'd rather be anywhere other than talking to the person or people in front of you.[5]

Memorability

What we've advised so far is all very well, but not much use if what you have to say to people seems to go in one ear and out the other. It is important to have techniques for making your communication memorable.

Firstly, think about the structure. Bear in mind that it's the start and end of any communication that's remembered most, whether it's a speech, presentation or an explanation – so don't sandwich the important part of what you have to say between a long winded, less relevant opening and finish. Again, there's an effective theory about this called the 'Primacy-Recency Effect'[6] to help you structure your message. It goes like this:

- Tell them what you're going to tell them
- Tell them
- Tell them what you told them.

The Primacy-Recency effect is also the reason why first impressions tend to stick. Make sure you make a good one, because it may be difficult to alter it at a later stage. Now, this shouldn't send you into a spin about whether people instantly like or dislike you — just remember that you'll always give a better impression by never pretending to be anything other than yourself! Relax, and you'll find whoever you're talking to will, too.

Don't make too many points. Research shows that our ability to retain information (memory) at any given time is limited. If too much is offered it either prevents us absorbing more or 'overwrites' what we're currently remembering! Stick to the most important points of your message rather than bombarding your audience with information and causing cerebral gridlock!

● THE EFFECTS OF COMMON PITFALLS

Here are things to watch out for and try to avoid:

Common Pitfalls	
Action	Effect
Objective/message is not clear	People don't 'get it', lose interest and become confused and bored.
Not adapted to audience/ not relevant	The message doesn't relate to the audience and they may therefore feel frustrated, bored and disengaged.
Lack of rapport	There is less willingness to warm to you and build trust, as well as less belief in the message. The audience may disengage.
Lack of credibility	The audience won't trust you or, therefore, buy in to your message, however persuasive you are.
Lack of confidence	Your lack of confidence can transmit to the audience and reduce their confidence in your message and likelihood of accepting what you're saying.
Incorrect tone or body language	Your message is diluted because your verbal and non-verbal cues are confusing or contradict the message.
Not memorable	Only parts of the message are remembered and they may not be the most important.
Making too many points	The audience may find it hard to remember everything, lose focus on the key points and may become bored or confused.
Repetition/fillers	The audience can become frustrated with hearing the same points over and over and your message becomes diluted. The audience may also stop listening.
Transactional analysis – use of Parent or Child approach	You may come across as either patronising (parent) or without enough gravitas to be taken seriously (child). Either way will result in the audience not taking your messages on board.

● GET YOUR STORY STRAIGHT

This exercise is designed to help you communicate your message effectively by sticking to the important points.

Step 1

Start by putting your communication into words. Your communication can be verbal or written and can take whatever form you like; for example a presentation, a letter or a chapter in a book.

Step 2

Next write a summary of your communication. This should be a written preview for the audience of no more than 30 words. As it's a summary, use full sentences and proper English.

> **Summary – 30 words**

Step 3

Once you have finished, review your original communication in light of your summary and delete any points from the original that are not in your summary.

This will enable you to think about the story behind your communication, while sticking only to the key points to get your message across. It'll make you focus and minimise repetition and digression. Don't worry if it takes you a bit of time at first, your communication will be more effective as a result...

In the words of George Bernard Shaw...

'I'm sorry to have written such a long letter, but I didn't have time to write a shorter one.'

● DO YOU AGREE WITH YOU?

This will help you develop your oral communication skills like presentations or speeches. It's easy to just read through the information we've given you and then think you're applying it. However, that rarely happens.

So, in this exercise you'll record your behaviour to see how you really do communicate. It will make you more aware of your style so you can make adjustments where appropriate, because many of us do things like using fillers without realising it. You can choose how to do the first step:

Step 1 – Video yourself

This would be ideal (using a camera, camcorder or mobile phone) to give you as much information as possible about how your presentation or speech sounds and looks. Once you've done it:

- Play the video back and rate your performance in each of the 'behaviours' in the table on page 54, using a scale of 1-4.
- Pretend you're someone in an audience, listening to you – would you be convinced?

- Ask someone whose opinion you'd value to watch your video and rate you using the table below.

If you don't want to film yourself, ask someone else to be your 'audience' and rate your performance using the table (following the steps above).

Key:

1. Very ineffective 2. Ineffective 3. Effective 4. Very effective

Video Ratings	
Behaviour	Rating 1-4
Is the message/story clear?	
Is it suited to the audience?	
Did you build rapport?	
Do you come across with credibility?	
Do you appear confident?	
Does your body language convey the right message?	
Do you seem to believe in what you're saying?	
Do you avoid looking directly at people?	
Did you use the Primacy-Recency effect to structure your story?	
Did you stick to a small number of important points?	
Is it relevant?	
Do you use repetition or fillers?	
Do you use an 'Adult' approach? (Transactional Analysis)	

Step 2 – Compare your ratings

Once you've rated yourself using the table above and/or asked someone else to do so, you'll have valuable information to help develop your methods of communication.

- Compare your own assessment with the way someone else rates you.
- Start by identifying what you could improve.
- If you have several things which you could improve, focus on only three at first because this will be manageable and you're more likely to make real progress than if you tackled everything at once – you can work on other things, next. Read through this tool again to find what's relevant to what you need most.
- If there are any discrepancies between your own and someone else's ratings, discuss it with them constructively by sharing and comparing opinions to make sure you know what you need to improve – and why.
- If someone else has rated you, ask them for any additional, general ideas about how you could communicate more effectively.
- Think about additional ways to learn about communication skills – talk to your line manager or coach about attending a workshop or other professional training – especially if you lack confidence, you'd be surprised how much fun it would be!
- If you have a 1 or 2 for the message/story being clear, then use the 'Get your story straight' exercise on page 53 to summarise your message and really clarify the important points you want to get across.

● FURTHER INFORMATION

If you found this tool useful then you are likely to find the following tools both insightful and relevant:

- How to be assertive
- How to influence others
- How to develop rapport
- How to actively listen
- How to communicate your vision.

● REFERENCES

1   Nabi, R. L., Roskos-Ewoldsen, D., & Carpentier, F. D. (2008). Subjective knowledge and fear appeal effectiveness: Implications for message design. Health communication, 23(2), 191-201.

2   Lewis, I., Watson, B., & Tay, R. (2007). Examining the effectiveness of physical threats in road safety advertising: The role of the third-person effect, gender, and age. Transportation Research Part F: Traffic Psychology and Behaviour, 10(1), 48-60.

3   Inamori, T., & Analoui, F. (2010). Beyond Pygmalion effect: the role of managerial perception. Journal of Management Development, 29(4), 306-321.

4   Van Cappellen, P., Corneille, O., Cols, S., & Saroglou, V. (2011). Beyond mere compliance to authoritative figures: Religious priming increases conformity to informational influence among submissive people. The International Journal for the Psychology of Religion, 21(2), 97-105.

5   Argyle, M., Alkema, F. & Gilmour, R. (1971). The communication of friendly and hostile attitudes by verbal and non-verbal signals. European Journal of Social Psychology, 1, 385-402 in Arnold, J., Cooper, C. & Roberston, I. (1998). Work Psychology. Prentice Hall.

6   Jones, E. et al (1968). Pattern of performance and ability attribution: An unexpected primacy effect. Journal of Personality and Social Psychology, 10, 317-340.

HOW TO ACTIVELY LISTEN

Understand what is meant by active listening and why it is important for effective communication.

● ISN'T IT INTERESTING?

You're at a party. It's busy. Inevitably, you find yourself in the kitchen. After all, that's where all great parties end up. You're talking to someone you've never met before and − despite the five or six other noisy conversations going on around you − following every word. A remarkable feat of listening skills. Or is it?

'Shaken…not stirred'

A long-standing phenomenon in psychology is known as the 'Cocktail party effect'.[1] It shows how our listening capacity, even in very busy situations such as a cocktail party, can be strong but is not entirely dependent on the words that we hear. We have an ability to pick out and listen to a single voice, in a crowd of voices, using the cues of physical differences as much as listening to the spoken words.

Differences such as gender,[2] intensity of voice and speaker location[3] all have a considerable impact on our ability to maintain attention on a single speaker in a crowded room. As soon as these important cues were removed, the listener quickly lost the ability to pay attention to the message. This in turn meant that they struggled to remember the point or anything about the person giving the message.

This tool can help

Listening clearly isn't just about hearing a few words and phrases. It involves engaging in understanding and deciphering the real message rather than selectively attending to information. This tool is all about how to actively listen and will help you to understand what is meant by active listening and why it is important for effective communication.

● INTRODUCTION

We've all been doing it for long enough – since the moment we were born, in fact – but most of us are not as good at it as we think we are. In psychological terms, listening is a 'cognitive process' – it involves thought, attention and awareness. It's the conscious mental process of giving meaning to the sounds we hear and 'contextualising' them. In other words, we interpret sounds in relation to other factors, including circumstance, emotion or habit.

It is said that 'we have two ears but only one mouth because listening is twice as hard as talking!'

Even so, many of us are still just pretending. Think about some of the conversations you've had which were more a matter of taking turns to speak, which is ironic, considering how much we all want to be listened to and understood!

While we can speak at 100 to 175 words per minute, we're able to listen intelligently at up to 300 words per minute.[4] As we all know, and doubtless find useful on occasion, this means we can 'listen' and think about all sorts of other things at the same time. However, 'listening with one ear' means that only part of our minds are paying attention, which is less useful and could be problematic, if it becomes habitual. This is where 'active listening' comes in – the difference is that it's **listening with a purpose.**

● WHAT IS ACTIVE LISTENING?

Active listening is a structured way of listening and responding to others in a way that improves mutual understanding, by focusing attention on the speaker. Its intent is to 'listen for meaning' and the listener checks with the speaker to ensure statements are correctly heard and understood.

In situations of conflict, people tend to concentrate more on what they are going to say next, than on listening to what's being said, which can mean they 'miss the point' of what is being said, adding misunderstanding or frustration to the interaction, rather than understanding or resolution.

Active listening constitutes three elements:

- Hearing – the process of capturing sound waves and sending this data to the brain.
- Interpreting – as information is received, the brain interprets the data according to previous experience, learning and other influences.
- Assigning a contextual meaning – the brain gives 'heard' data specific meaning, according to situation or circumstance.

For example, someone might say: **'I need the rolls now'.**

Depending on the circumstances in which these words are heard, you could interpret them to mean:

1. It's someone talking to their chauffeur.
   Meaning: **Rolls Royce.**

2. Service at your local Chinese restaurant is particularly slow, tonight.
   Meaning: **Spring rolls.**

3. You are practising for a rock show and you are speaking to your drummer.
   Meaning: **Drum rolls.**

So, meaning is determined 'contextually'!

● WHY IS ACTIVE LISTENING IMPORTANT?

Studies of relationships in the workplace consistently reveal that staff often feel their managers don't listen to them. The role of manager can be hectic because of the need to assimilate information from different sources, quickly. Too often, it means insufficient time is given to listening to what is really being said.

The benefits of active listening include encouraging people to 'open up', avoiding misunderstandings, resolving conflict and building trust. It's also key to picking up information which might otherwise be overlooked.

What gets in the way of active listening?

Because we think a lot faster than someone can speak, our minds wander as we listen. In all communication, there are barriers between 'sender' and 'receiver' which hinder the process. However, just being aware of them will help you listen more effectively:

There are four types of barriers to listening:[5]

1. Psychological
   This may include fear, prejudice or lack of interest. For example, if you work in marketing you're probably not as interested in the company's annual figures as the finance director (but desperate to know how your presentation went). It's about how or whether what is being said impacts your day-to-day activities or interests.

2. Physical
   Disability, fatigue or ill health on the part of the listener. For example, suffering a cold, with blocked sinuses and streaming eyes is not conducive to listening to anyone, at all.

3. Environmental
   Distracting noises, uncomfortable seating, or an overheated, stuffy room.

4. Expectation
   Expecting this afternoon's talk to be really boring! Anticipating bad news. Being spoken to in confusing jargon.

● HOW CAN I IMPROVE MY ACTIVE LISTENING SKILLS?

It's relatively easy to manage or resolve the tangible, physical or environmental barriers, but more difficult to deal with internal ones. However, preparing adequately for discussions and meetings will do much to overcome them.

Here are some 'active listening' techniques, based on the three elements of the listening process we mentioned at the start — hearing, interpreting and contextualising.

Hearing and interpreting

- First of all, stop talking, or at least pause to invite the other person to speak!
- Eliminate as many distractions as possible, both external and internal.
- Control your own non-verbal signals to the speaker. Pay attention to how you're standing or sitting, your eye contact and small encouragements like nodding, smiling and mirroring the speaker's own body language (obviously, this doesn't mean behaving like a budgie with a mirror — just adopt an empathetic or complementary attitude). Be discreet, too, about eye contact — while it's important to appear open and receptive, take care not to look as if you're staring or appearing inquisitorial! (It's as well, too, to note that interpretation of eye contact varies amongst cultures.)

Research has shown that we can put a lot more emphasis on body language (55%) or tone of voice (38%) than on the actual words (7%) when we are interpreting ambiguous messages. That means that HOW something is said, and HOW speakers hold themselves can reveal more than WHAT they say.[6]

Understanding

- Make sure you understand the purpose of the speaker, and also be aware of what you want from the conversation.
- Ask questions (without interrupting) and use notes you have written to remind you what needs clarifying.
- You can also try 'reflecting'. This is used a lot by sales professionals. What we say can be separated into three types of information — facts, thoughts (or beliefs) and feelings (or emotions). 'Reflecting' means repeating back to someone what they have said (or suggested) to check or demonstrate that you have understood. You can 'reflect' emotions, too, for example: '....so, this has left you feeling confused?'
- Take notes. Write down key words and phrases to jog your memory later.
- Summarise or paraphrase what you understand to be the facts you're given; for example, **'As I understand it, what you're saying is....'** or **'So your point is that....'** This gives you both an opportunity to verify or correct understanding.

Practise being a good listener at any opportunity, in a shop, over dinner or with friends.

- Share thoughts or beliefs that you have heard, and try to convey the underlying feelings or emotions which you believe are involved. For example, the speaker may be very upset and wants you to display empathy or sympathy with their situation. It is this reflection of thought and feelings which distinguishes reflecting from just parroting back to the speaker, which might get a bit tedious and annoying for all concerned.

● SELF ASSESSMENT

Completing these statements will identify your listening habits, and indicate where you might improve.

Active Listening Self Assessment Tool

1. When I have difficulty hearing I...

2. When I have difficulty understanding what a speaker means I...

3. When I agree with a speaker's message, I usually...

4. When I disagree with a speaker's message, I usually...

5. My responsibility as a listener in any situation is...

6. As I listen to someone speak I do the following to help myself understand the message...

7. The most important thing that I know about listening is...

● NEXT STEPS

By now you should have a greater sense of what active listening involves and how you can start to consider your approach. Below are some suggestions for practical next steps following on from this tool:

Review the self assessment tool

Review what you have written above to identify your strengths and weaknesses. Your strengths will be the kinds of thing you do automatically, but your weaknesses may be what you rarely or never do, and could now practise.

Look for opportunities to practise

Think of opportunities that occur in your current work or elsewhere, to practise. You may want to consider situations where you have to interact with other people, whether one-to-one or in group meetings.

Active listening feedback exercise

Ask someone you trust, for example your mentor, line manager or colleague to present you with 10 minutes' information about a particular subject. If possible, ask a third party to observe. After the 10 minutes, summarise what you've heard. Apart from recounting facts, try saying things like: 'What I understand is that...'. Then ask both the speaker and observer to comment on how much you were able to pick up.

Observe others

Ask others how they actively listen. Explain what you mean and are looking for, using the information in this tool to help you. Observe them and see first hand what they do well or not so well.

Repeat the exercise a month later, having re-read this tool, to check your progress and use some of the techniques we've talked about. Watch other people 'listening,' too!

● FURTHER INFORMATION

If you found this tool useful then you are likely to find the following tools both insightful and relevant:

- How to communicate effectively
- How to develop rapport
- How to manage difficult conversations
- How to give feedback.

● REFERENCES

1   Conway, A. R., Cowan, N., & Bunting, M. F. (2001). The cocktail party phenomenon revisited: The importance of working memory capacity. **Psychonomic Bulletin & Review**, 8(2), 331-335.

2   Koch, I., Lawo, V., Fels, J., & Vorländer, M. (2011). Switching in the cocktail party: Exploring intentional control of auditory selective attention. **Journal of Experimental Psychology: Human Perception and Performance**, 37(4), 1140.

3   Noble, W., and Perret, S. (2002). 'Hearing speech against spatially separate competing speech versus competing noise,' Perception Psychophysics. 64, 1325–1336.

4   Manktelow, J. (2003). **Introduction to Memory Techniques**, London and New York: Routledge

5   De Boer, J. (2006). **Better results with active listening**. UK Training Articles.

6   Mehrabian, A. (1981). **Silent messages: Implicit communication of emotions and attitudes** (2nd ed.). Wadsworth, Belmont, California.

HOW TO MANAGE YOUR IMPACT

Understand the type of impact you would like to achieve in various situations. Evaluate your own style, learn why it can be ineffective and find out how to develop your approach to create a different impact.

● ISN'T IT INTERESTING?

Two billion years ago a meteorite 10km in diameter hit the earth southwest of Johannesburg, South Africa, creating an enormous crater – the Vredefort Dome. The impact would have vaporised about 70km^3 of rock and may have increased the earth's oxygen levels to a degree that made the development of multicellular life possible…

It's all about style

Now that's an impact. So how can you make an impact?

Our style: the way we act, dress, behave and talk all have a significant influence on how we are perceived and evaluated by others. The trick is to be able to adjust your approach to suit the situation. The style you use to present information is what often determines the impact you make, described below.

Minority influence

In the late 1960s, Moscovici conducted a series of experiments[1] looking into the way in which certain individuals had the power to influence the thinking and beliefs of future generations. His studies into innovation and creativity and the power of the few to influence others led him to pinpoint a certain behavioural style that an individual or minority must adapt in order to be able to influence a majority view.

In a simple experiment, Moscovici showed some participants with normal vision a coloured slide and asked them to indicate its colour and brightness. The participants were asked to do this 36 times in a sequence, each time being shown the same blue slide. Moscovici set up three different conditions, each with 6 participants:

1. There were 4 real participants and 2 paid confederates who were instructed to call the slides green instead of blue on all trials.

2. The 2 paid confederates were instructed to call the slides green on approximately 2/3 of the trials and in random order.

3. There were no paid confederates.

The minority only influenced the view of the real participants in the first condition; surprisingly 8.5% of real participants changed their view and called the slides green and 32% of the real participants reported having seen green slides at least once.

Moscovici concluded that for a minority to have an impact they have to be active and consistent and this leads others within the group to perceive them as more confident and competent.

This tool can help

At times, everyone questions whether they will be able to create their desired impact. This tool is about how to manage your impact and will help you better understand the type of impact you would like to achieve in various situations. It also helps you to evaluate your own style, why it can be ineffective and how to develop your approach to create the impact you would like to have.

● WHY IS IMPACT IMPORTANT?

Impact is important at work. Regardless of your intention it will be the impact of your behaviour and what you say that people will identify with and act upon. As impact is not necessarily linked to intention. This means it can be difficult to pin down and may be controversial at times.

Ask yourself, 'how aware am I of the impact I have on other people?' You may find that although you think you understand your impact the reality might be less clear cut. Follow this question up with the same one to those around you to see whether there is a difference. The difference between what you meant and how it was received in a given situation can lead to different reactions and behaviours from those around you. For example, it could mean developing trust in a relationship and being effective, or developing an ineffective relationship that leads to those around you being more challenging than they might have been otherwise.

This reality can highlight the importance of impact. Awareness of impact can lead to better understanding and appreciation in your transactions with others. Below is a step-by-step account to get you started on developing your impact.

The next page outlines a four-stage process to manage your impact:

1. Develop self-awareness

2. Identify your desired impact

3. Act

4. Evaluation.

● THE IMPACT PENDULUM

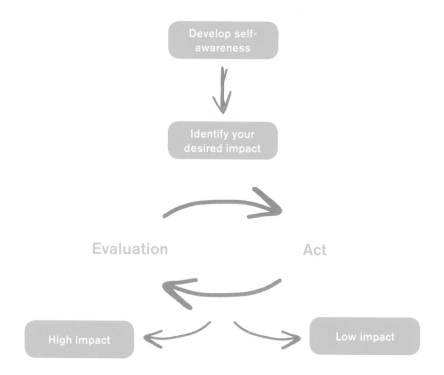

● STAGES OF IMPACT

Stage 1– Develop self-awareness

To begin to develop your impact you need 'self-awareness' of your effect on other people. Choose someone who you have the opportunity to make a more positive impact on than you do at present. This could be a manager, a colleague, a customer or indeed someone in your personal life. Ask yourself:

- What do I know about my own impact on them?
- How do they perceive me?
- Why am I motivated to better understand my impact on this person?

Asking yourself the above questions can help you to understand what you think you know, what the reality is and why you want to change your impact on this person.

Stage 2 – Identify your desired impact

The next stage will be to try to identify what type of impact you would like to have on this person. You can do this by identifying an individual who you perceive to have a positive impact on others. The key questions you should ask yourself about this person are:

- What do they do that makes a positive impact?
- What is the outcome of their positive impact?
- If they had a similar style to me, how would the impact have been different?
- Which types of people or situations do I find most difficult to have a positive impact on?

It is necessary to understand the factors that can make a difference in terms of impact on a particular person and/or situation. This means that the characteristics of any given situation need to be attended to so that you can adapt your style in line with that need. For example, in a particular situation are you able to identify what is working and what is not? Gaining a better understanding of what your impact actually is will enable you to compare this with your intended impact. This will enable you to realign what you are intending your impact to be and what the reality is.

Stage 3 – Act

See what happens. Your impact is affected by your desire and ability to read the person. There are a number of factors that you should attend to:

- Ensure you are adopting an open, positive body language – smiling and nodding helps to show understanding.

- Ask questions to clarify your understanding.

- Summarise statements to check your understanding as this will encourage the individual to feel as though they are being listened to and that you are interested in their thoughts and ideas.

- Use this impact tool to develop your impact to enable you to influence, motivate, inspire and persuade others.

- Adapt your style when interacting with different people and situations to ensure you have maximum impact. This can be based on the desired outcomes and the style that you feel will be most influential on them. This means that your style is fluid. If you re-evaluate the style you are using you can adjust it if it is not having the desired outcome.

Stage 4 – Evaluation

There is a need to reflect upon a situation during, as well as after. Initially this will need to occur consciously; however, later this will become easier and more like second nature for you. This will require you to assess:

- Why did you choose that particular method in that situation or with that person?

- Did you achieve what you wanted to in this situation/with this person?

- Did you get feedback about your impact during and after the transaction?

These questions will help you to identify the key elements that made, or could have made, a positive impact. You could have a more positive impact by evaluating and consciously choosing to use key elements that would help you improve your impact. This stage feeds back into the act stage. You can try to adapt your style to modify your approach and make a more positive impact.

After a period of time you can re-evaluate an interaction where you were attending to your impact to help you to explore what went well and what you could have done better. Ask yourself:

- What were the barriers and challenges in that situation to create a positive impact?

- Do other people find these factors to be barriers or challenges?

- How could you overcome these barriers/how do others overcome these barriers or challenges?

- Are you having as much impact as your skill level suggests you might?

- If not, why not? What could be stopping you from having a positive impact?

Feedback is essential to help you to understand and make changes to your preferred style to better suit others or the task in hand. If you ask for feedback to help improve your impact style, then this is initially most useful when gained from situations when no conflict was involved.

● WAYS TO IMPROVE YOUR IMPACT ON OTHERS

Matching their body language

This can be done to build rapport and many people do it naturally to ensure they blend or fit in. It can include adopting a similar posture, giving the same amount of eye contact and matching others' hand gestures in speed and frequency. The intention behind body matching is to share and understand the other person's experience of the world, as how we use our body influences our emotional state. Although these factors are subtle they are attended to by us and others, even if subconsciously, and will affect our impact on others.

Voice matching

Again we naturally adapt our voice in volume and pace to that of others. For example, when dealing with someone who is really passionate about something, this can be catching and we can feel excited and passionate about it also. The converse is true when dealing with people who are angry, where we can match them slightly below their level of volume and speed. Then we can influence them by gradually lowering our own voice or slowing the pace and this can lead to them doing the same.

Mismatching

This is the opposite of matching and is a useful skill. It aims to be disengaging and can be used to bring the discussion to a close. It need not invalidate the other person or their view.

Cross-over matching

This involves less concentration and focus than matching, as we would match the other person's body language with a different type of movement; for example, tapping a foot in time to their rhythm of speech. Again this can help build our non-verbal relationship with the person and can be used to calm or slow the situation subconsciously.

These factors will further enhance your understanding of the impact your behaviour and actions have on others and how you can adapt your style to improve your own impact.

Creating a positive impact is something that requires a fairly high level of self-awareness. You should try to gain the views of people around you and identify the impact of your behaviour in different situations. Principally you need to understand the impact of your approach on other people, in order to make a positive difference.

Continual feedback is needed to help you understand your impact on others. There are a number of ways to ensure that what you intended and the reality of your impact are aligned. These include:

- Request to have 360 degree feedback to understand the perspectives of those around you.
- Have regular and informal feedback sessions.
- Create a clear development plan to improve your impact in progressively difficult situations, or with difficult individuals.

Critical factors in creating a positive impact

Flexibility

It is crucial that you are able to listen to and observe the individual vigilantly. Pay particular attention to the situation and try to see it from their perspective.

Immediate impact

It is critical to manage the initial three minutes, as during this time your impact is attended to most by the other person and impressions are formed. These impressions can be difficult to overcome, so it is best to ensure our impact is as we intend it to be during this time. Do this by building rapport, listening and sharing information to help increase your approachability.

Attend to non-verbal behaviour

Be aware of your own and the other person's behaviours. This will give you the awareness of how they are feeling so you can adapt accordingly to increase your positive impact.

● IMPACT MANAGEMENT TOOL

This exercise will help you with the evaluation stage of the model described earlier. Doing so will enable you to identify themes relating to high or low impact and therefore help you to modify your approach.

Step 1

Think about two situations, one where you had a high impact and one where your impact was low.

- For example, a high-impact situation might be when you did a presentation that blew people away!

- A low-impact situation might be when you put together a business case that people were not persuaded by.

Step 2

Answer the questions below with each of these situations in mind.

Impact Management Tool	High Impact	Low Impact
The situation		
● Who was involved (e.g. the audience)? ● What did I hope to achieve? ● What approach did I take? ● Why did I take this approach?		
What were the highs:		
● What worked well? ● What aspects of the situation made me feel good? ● Why? ● What positive feedback did I get?		

Impact Management Tool	High Impact	Low Impact
What were the lows: • What didn't work well? • What aspects of the situation made me feel disheartened? • Why? • What negative feedback did I get?		
Identify a role model: • What would they have done that would have had a more positive impact? • Why would they have done that? • How is my approach/behaviour different from the role model?		
Reflection: • What were the key elements to creating a positive impact? • How can I optimise this behaviour again? • What were the barriers and challenges to creating a more positive impact? • How could I overcome these barriers? • How could I have improved my impact in this situation? • What would I have achieved by doing this? • What support do I need to help me create a more positive impact?		
Feedback: • What feedback have I received on my impact? • What have I done with this information? • How has this changed my behaviour?		

Step 3

Review the situations that you have described in the table above. Identify any themes relating to you having a high impact or any relating to you having a low impact. This will identify the approaches that you are using.

Insert the high- and low-impact themes from Steps 1 and 2 into the Impact Management Matrix on the next page, according to their impact and how often you use them.

The matrix will then indicate whether you should: stop doing this, start doing this, continue with what you are doing or ignore it.

● IMPACT MANAGEMENT MATRIX

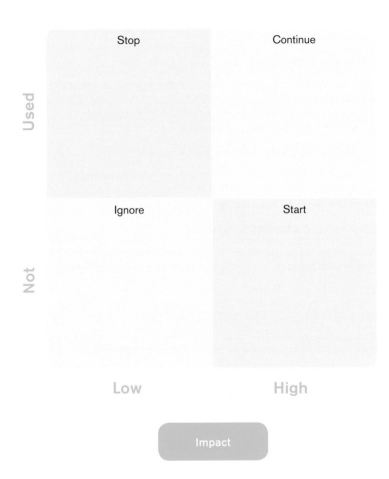

● NEXT STEPS

Now that you have considered the factors involved in managing your impact and have some practical tools to consider, it is worth thinking about what to do next. Here are a number of suggestions to maintain momentum (although these are by no means exhaustive):

Look for opportunities to practise

Think about the opportunities that you have in your current work, or beyond, where you can practise role modelling good behaviour or improving your profile.

Talk to your role model

Consider someone you know who has a positive impact on those around them. Think about what it is particularly that you think is great about them or their approach. You may then want to think about how you compare. This may seem daunting if you feel that there is a big gap but this is the starting point for you to develop a plan to improve. Think about what your role model would do to have a positive impact and whether you would also use this approach. Think about any successful approaches they use that you are not currently using. You could also discuss your impact management matrix with them.

Write a development plan

Use the tool in this document to highlight your approach to managing your impact. Once you have established how you go about creating a positive impact you could put together a focused development plan to improve your effectiveness. Ensure that you put in time to review this in the future, in order to measure your progress.

Gather feedback on existing performance

You may find it useful to benchmark your current performance by asking for formal or informal feedback. This can help you understand how you can help others around you and where people would like you to be more visible.

Look for opportunities to practise

Think about the opportunities that you have in your current work, or beyond, where you can practise managing your impact and making a positive impression.

● FURTHER INFORMATION

If you found this tool useful then you are likely to find the following tools both insightful and relevant:

- How to develop rapport
- How to raise energy levels
- How to be assertive
- How to build and maintain trust.

● REFERENCES

1   Moscovici, S. Lage, E. & Naffrenchoux, M. (1969). Influences of a consistent minority on the responses of a majority in a colour perception task, **Sociometry**, 32, 365-80.

HOW TO MANAGE DIFFICULT CONVERSATIONS

Deal with situations where you have to discuss something awkward or deal with challenging people.

● ISN'T IT INTERESTING?

Raise your hand

Think back to your school days when you're in a class with your teacher and he or she asks your class a particularly difficult question and you have to put your hand up if you think the answer is a), b) or c). How many people would make up their mind independently and how many would base their decision on what other people say? In 1956, Solomon Asch conducted experiments into conformity.[1]

Have you got the measure?

Asch asked groups of people to vote out loud on which line was the same length as the one on the left.

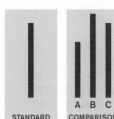

STANDARD COMPARISON

In each group there was one real participant and several stooges who had been told to give the obviously incorrect answer 'c'. Shockingly, 75% of people went along with the majority vote on at least one occasion despite the answer being clearly wrong. When questioned as to why they did this, participants explained a 'pressure' to conform.

This has been demonstrated in more modern settings, for example in a mock-jury activity[2] participants were required to pass judgement on how much a widow of a farmer should inherit from his estate instead of his sister. When individually asked, around 70% gave her less than half of the estate; however, when placed in a jury, the joint decision increased this to more than 95%. This is a clear case of a majority causing the minority to conform, leading to a skewed decision.

This tool can help

Some of the most difficult conversations you will have at work are those where you are going against the majority opinion, and feel pressured to conform. This tool is about how to manage difficult conversations and will help you to approach and be successful in going against the majority, and other kinds of difficult conversations that can hinder you at work.

● INTRODUCTION

Occasionally, you're bound to have difficult conversations – telling your partner you crashed their car, perhaps, or dealing with an underperforming employee. However, when you know how to manage these conversations, you can dispel some of the tension you and the other parties may feel.

What is 'difficult' is different for everyone, but it's often:

- Giving a performance appraisal to a problem employee
- Saying 'no' to a colleague or manager
- Confronting unreasonable behaviour
- Disagreeing with the majority
- Admitting to a mistake.

While the details of different difficult conversations vary, there are valuable techniques and tips which can apply to any of them, because our reasons for avoiding them are often the same.

What is a difficult conversation?

The examples below can cause conversations to be difficult, generally by increasing the level of stress and/or tension in one or both of the parties involved.

- Fear of rejection
- Embarrassment
- Feelings of anger
- Feelings of injustice.

● WHY DO WE AVOID DIFFICULT CONVERSATIONS?

Past experience

Memories of a single difficult conversation can affect our attitude to even the possibility of subsequent ones, on any subject. Such memories can make us go to great lengths to avoid confrontation of any kind – or to react with the ferocity of a cornered rat. No matter which behaviour you recognise in yourself, you can learn to handle things with elegance and cool!

Focus on the positive

Think about the approaches you have taken in the past that worked well. After all, a top athlete who competed in the long jump wouldn't spend all his time worrying about his proficiency in the 100 metres! No, he would spend his time working on the thing he does best – the long jump. Work out what your long jump is.

Fear of emotional reactions

This is common, whether the emotional reaction is our own or others'. Try to put yourself in the other person's shoes and deliver your message in a way that's clear, but not damaging. In a difficult performance appraisal, for example, it's important that the employee understands what is unacceptable but also feels advised or guided rather than merely criticised. Fear of your own emotional reactions is also common.

Try to anticipate any emotional reactions you may have

Think about how you will recognise them when they start to appear (e.g. will you feel a tense feeling in your stomach, or a burning feeling in your throat?). Increasing your awareness of your emotional states will help you manage them when they do occur. If you find yourself becoming overwhelmed with emotions then be honest with the person you are speaking with and explain how the situation is making you feel.

Fear of feeling bad

Often we don't talk about sensitive issues with someone, because we're worried it'll make them feel bad about themselves but, while this may appear kind or polite, it's more to do with our own fear of not being liked in return!

Part of conquering this fear is recognising that giving these difficult messages to people is not a negative event

The reason you are giving the message is to improve the situation. Focus on the positive reasons for the conversation and you will gain the confidence of the person you are talking to.

Fear of making the problem worse/retribution

Fear of making the problem worse and inviting retribution stems from a fear of being thought incompetent. Confidence in your own ability to deal with a situation comes mostly from knowing why you need to do so, in the first place.

Focus on the positive reasons for approaching this situation and this attitude will shine through

Isn't it easier just to put up with it?

Well, yes…but no. The consequences of doing nothing can be far worse than any momentary qualms you might have when you just deal with stuff!

● WHY WE SHOULDN'T AVOID DIFFICULT CONVERSATIONS

Avoiding difficult conversations at work might be the convenient approach, but you're less likely to get the best outcome. Here are some reasons not to avoid a difficult conversation.

Worsening of the situation

Left unaddressed, difficult situations (such as unreasonable behaviour) can get worse. If people aren't given feedback about the impact of their behaviour they're unlikely to change. Also, your resentment or irritation will probably increase or even lead to some outburst which, at best, you'll regret or, at worst, could be extremely detrimental, both immediately and long-term.

Poor relationships cost money

If relationships break down because no one's addressing a particular issue, one or more of those involved may even quit their jobs, with obvious financial and other consequences. Or, in situations where people want to leave but feel unable or disinclined to, the effect on productivity can be less immediate, but more damaging over time. People express distress or dissatisfaction at work in all kinds of ways, from withdrawing socially, working to rule or ('oops!...') wiping a database, and worse….

'Groupthink'

This is when the majority view or behaviour in a group inhibits individuals within it from voicing or acting on their own better judgement. The causes of major disasters are often traced back to someone who 'thought something wasn't quite right about that, surely?' but said or did nothing.

Vilification

Allowing your own or others' 'bad feeling' to fester can spiral from being annoying or uncomfortable, to seriously damaging , even to the point – when such a situation occurs at managerial level – of actively resisting or quashing rivals' suggestions, from which the entire company could benefit.

● THE 'PREPARE, ADDRESS, FOLLOW-UP' APPROACH

To successfully manage a difficult conversation, it's important to fully prepare for it. The model below provides a simple and useful 'map' for preparing for, and conducting our trickier encounters, and then following them up – or smoothing things out afterwards.

It's important, too, to separate out the two different elements of the conversation: 'what happened', (for example: 'I heard you say something about the way so-and-so looked, at work') and 'how do you feel about that' (for example: 'it made me feel uncomfortable'). Try to filter out the emotional aspects but still be honest about how you're feeling.

Here is more detailed advice to help you with this approach:

Prepare

Impact	Think about what impact the situation has had on you, and be honest about this. For more info see 'How to manage your impact' tool.
Strategy	Consider the following: ● Who do you need to talk to? ● When would be the best time to talk to them? ● What do you want to achieve? ● What is the context? (for example, there's no point in asking for a raise when profits are at an all-time low)
Key messages	Think about the key messages you want to get across. Prepare about three to take to your discussion.
Secondary	Prepare a secondary goal. For example, if you go in aiming for a pay rise, have a secondary target, or 'plan B' of arranging a pay review in three months' time.
Anticipate	If you want a pay review, try to anticipate what responses you might get. If it's a more interpersonal issue, try to be a bit empathetic; in other words, think about how the other person might be feeling when you talk to them.

Address

Acknowledge differences	Acknowledge, openly, that both parties have differences. Bring them out into the open for discussion.
Be honest and direct	Don't be afraid to give a direct message, as long as you're not aggressive or emotional. This way, you'll come across as objective, and often people appreciate knowing where they stand.
Partnership	Make the other person feel you're asking them to work with you to solve the problem – don't sound as if you're telling them off, or what to do.
Responsibility	Take responsibility for your role in the situation.
Assertive	Be assertive. Don't allow them to fob you off – insist on confronting the issue. For more information, see the 'How to be assertive' tool.
Private	Make sure you meet them in private. Otherwise, you run the risk of them feeling you're trying to undermine or humiliate them in front of colleagues.
Know when to stop	It's important to know where your boundaries are. It is not your responsibility to force someone into action. In the end, all you can do is make sure they hear and understand your message.

Follow up

Monitor progress	Ensure you monitor the progress of a situation, if appropriate (for instance if the difficult conversation is with someone you manage). Schedule a follow-up meeting and agree goals.
Maintain good feeling	Make an effort to maintain or create good feeling between you and the person concerned after the conversation – especially if it became heated.
Revisit	Revisit the conversation if necessary.

● NEXT STEPS

The best next step is to identify the most difficult conversations that you have coming up. Take a moment to think about whether the difficulty lies in the people involved or the topic of discussion, or a combination.

Use the PAF technique for each conversation. Don't expect the perfect outcome every time you have a difficult conversation, but do make time afterwards to review what did go well and how you might build on this the next time you face a similar conversation.

● FURTHER INFORMATION

If you found this tool useful then you are likely to find the following tools both insightful and relevant:

- How to be assertive
- How to communicate effectively
- How to actively listen
- How to manage your impact
- How to build and maintain trust
- How to give feedback
- How to reframe problems
- How to make reasoned judgements
- How to challenge others effectively.

● REFERENCES

1   Asch, S. (1956). Studies of independence and conformity: A minority of one against a unanimous majority. Psychological Monographs, 70.

2   Parkinson, S., & Baddeley, M. (2011). Group Decision-making: An Economic Analysis of Social Influence and Individual Difference in Experimental Juries, University of Cambridge.

BUILDING

HOW TO CREATE TEAM IDENTITY

Understand the factors behind building cohesion in your team.

● ISN'T IT INTERESTING?

How many zebras do you see in this picture?

So what is going on in this picture?

Looking at the picture, it's hard to pick out individual zebras; the zebra stripe patterns all look very similar. Sometimes it can be difficult to pick out individual people too, especially in groups we're not part of. Our brains have a limited capacity to make sense of the world,[1] so we take mental shortcuts and make generalisations, e.g. all young people wearing  'hoodies' cause trouble, so we avoid them. We see the nuance and differences in our own group much more easily; so whereas the Prime Minister will find it easy to differentiate between all politicians, we may find it less so.

Stars or stripes?

Zebra stripes take advantage of the fact that we find it more difficult to differentiate in groups that we are not part of.

For observers outside of the zebra herd, when zebras huddle together, their stripes act as a form of camouflage by making it difficult to pick out a target. The group identity is so strong that it can be difficult to differentiate individual members. Nature uses this principle for survival; the mass of patterns act as a deterrence to predators such as lions who attack isolated zebras.

Interestingly though, within a herd, the stripes actually help zebras to identify each other. Stripe patterns are individual, like fingerprints, and help zebras to keep track of offspring and distinguish members of their own herd from another.

This tool can help

Interestingly, in the picture you see a tactic that is used for survival. In today's globalised and technological corporate world, it is important for organisations to have a strong team identity to stay ahead of competitors and reach their consumers. This tool is about how to create team identity and will assist you in understanding the factors behind building cohesion in your team.

● WHO AM I?

Understanding your team is fundamental to getting the best from it, because your knowledge of its members' different skills and preferred methods of working will enable each to play to his or her strengths and overcome weaknesses.

Who am I? Social Identity Theory (SIT)[2]

There has been a large amount of research since the 1970s into how people identify themselves in a social context, with much of it coming under the label of 'Social Identity Theory'. In work environments how people do this can be of great importance because social interaction is key to an integrated and productive workforce. While many managers can be perfectly aware of the skills and traits of their workers, for example who is a 'team player' and who works better on their own, understanding their identity can often take a back seat.

In a modern piece of research[3] psychologists briefed participants who were either assigned to an imaginary team with strong definitions or one with weak definitions. Those who had strong definitions were more likely to identify with the theoretical group; additionally, they believed those in the group were like themselves, and looked more favourably on their actions. This was regardless of the ethnic, gender or any other group identity of the participant.

To summarise, 'Social Identity Theory' reveals that in successfully functioning groups, a shared identity provides cohesion amongst otherwise separate and different people. Obvious examples of 'group identity' include nationalities, cultures, religions and so on. And the people in your team are also a group, whose success depends on how strongly they feel about that – or whether they think they're a team at all.

Who am I at the moment? Self-Categorisation Theory (SCT)[4]

Simply, this is an individual's choice to behave according to his or her personal identity, or that of a group's 'shared identity'. Influencing factors will include what regard someone has for the group concerned, or how membership of it enhances self-esteem or conveys other benefits.

We've very briefly summarised two theories, so that when you create a team, or consider one which is already operational, you may have a better understanding of group formation and identity, and its possible impact on its members.

Next, we'll describe a model for creating team identity and practical steps for managing its various aspects.

● CREATING TEAM IDENTITY

The Pearn Kandola model of creating team identity

Simply bringing a group of people together and calling them a team doesn't make them one. They need to develop mutual trust, cooperation, support and commitment – in other words, a shared identity. If you can't identify ways in which your team is different from other groups in the organisation, it has no identity.

Here are the nine key elements necessary to successfully create team identity:

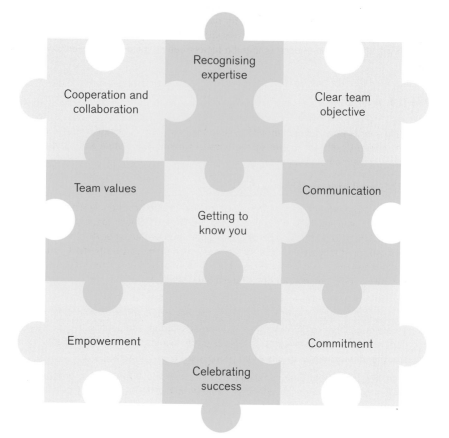

● THE MODEL EXPLAINED

Area	Explanation
Clear team objective	**What has the team been brought together to achieve?** Unless you can communicate the team's objectives clearly, there's little chance it'll understand why it's been formed at all! Ideally, members should have an opportunity to define the goals themselves, because they're more likely to develop objectives that they understand and believe they'll benefit from.
Recognising expertise	**What does each team member bring to the team?** We all benefit from regular, positive reinforcement of ourselves and acceptance by others. That's why a sense of team membership and identity is so important. Team membership tells us which groups of people we are accepted by and have similar values to our own, reinforcing our sense of identity and wellbeing.

Area	Explanation
Team values	**How are we going to work together?** One aspect that differentiates one team from another is its method of achieving goals. To help team members develop a sense of identity, as well as ownership and responsibility for the team as a whole, you need to give them time and space to outline and agree team values.
Cooperation and collaboration	**How are we going to support each other?** People who work independently to achieve a goal are often mistakenly called a team because they have the same goal and might meet regularly to discuss progress. However, an effective team is a group of people who collaborate to achieve a shared goal. In this way, effective team members are those focused on achieving the team goals rather than merely completing work allocated to them. Typically, people in teams who work collaboratively look for opportunities to help one another in undertaking the work assigned to them.
Getting to know you	**How well do your team members know each other?** **How can you help develop these relationships?** Getting to know one another helps to reinforce a sense of connection between team members which, in turn, reinforces team identity. Although it may feel as though this stage produces no clear output, it is key to increasing levels of mutual trust amongst team members and provides opportunities for them to either consciously or subconsciously agree effective ways of communicating. This increased contact, especially when informal, helps members understand each others' view of the team, which makes dealing with any conflict easier.
Communication	**How can you make sure that team members are communicating effectively?** The 'importance of communication' has become something of a cliché in organisations, but there's a reason for this. The way we communicate reveals a lot about us as individuals, and how well a team works. People often overrate their effectiveness in communicating, perhaps because it seems a 'given'. However, there are ways to ensure your team communicates effectively which, in turn, will help increase their sense of team membership and team identity.
Empowerment	**Making sure your team members take control** If you find yourself telling your team members what to do and how to do it, the chances are it's not a proper team. Instead, you've simply brought together a group of people to do your work – that's delegation. Neither can you simply tell the team what needs doing and leave them to it – that's laissez faire management! Empowerment is about genuinely giving people responsibility for what they do and how they do it, while providing support and guidance where necessary. With this approach, people are encouraged to work as a team because they recognise their responsibility to deliver. They also have the freedom to debate, try new approaches and take chances, knowing that their team mates will support them.
Celebrating success	**How do I make the most of what we are doing?** One of the easiest ways to maintain team identity is to ensure that progress and success are overtly recognised and celebrated. This helps team members recognise that the efforts they make and the work they do together is recognised. This helps not only to reinforce their feeling valued, but also to recognise the success of the team.

Area	Explanation
Commitment	**Why are team members committed to one team and not another?** Commitment is simple. It boils down to whether your team members: <ul><li>Accept and agree with what the team is doing.</li><li>Accept and agree how the team is doing what it needs to do.</li><li>Are willing to make an effort on behalf of the team.</li><li>Have the desire to remain a team member – what's in it for them?</li></ul> Getting all the previous 8 areas correct should leave your team members feeling motivated, valued and as though they're genuinely working towards achieving something of value. All this adds up to a sense of commitment to the team because its members will, often unconsciously, weigh up whether it's of benefit to them to continue being part of it, or whether it's become something they resent.

● PRACTICAL GUIDE TO TEAM ACTIVITIES

Clear team objective

If you have an overall objective, or mission, put this to the group and explain why it is important for you and for the organisation. Then ask the team to discuss their perceptions and understanding of what needs to be achieved. It is critical at this early stage that each member is absolutely certain about what needs to be achieved, why and for what benefit to the organisation, the team and themselves. Once all this is understood, you can throw the discussion open so that they can identify specifics.

Recognising expertise

An important way of creating team identity is making sure that every member understands:

- Why they have been selected as a team member.
- The role they are expected to play; that is, what skills, knowledge, experience or attitude they bring, which is of value to the team.
- The expertise other team members bring. This helps individuals develop mutual trust.

In doing this, be careful not to overplay or exaggerate people's expertise because if they subsequently fail to live up to your 'PR' you'll also lose credibility! You may also have inexperienced people on your team – encourage other members to identify learning opportunities for their new colleagues. This may also help to reduce anxiety about potential new people joining the team.

Team values

Try asking your team to debate and agree key questions about how they will work together, such as:

- What is the best way for the team to communicate? Is it face-to-face meetings? Teleconferences? Emails? A mixture? What type of things need to be communicated? How much communication is too much? Or too little?

- How will team members ensure they complete work they are allocated to deadline? What will happen if they don't?

- What are the expected standards of work? Is it that work should be drafted and brought to the next meeting to review as a group, or should work be completed to the final stage, before being presented?

- What support do the team members need to achieve their goals? Who is responsible for securing that support? How can team members support one another?

Once they have discussed and agreed the right approach for the team, their agreement also constitutes a kind of contract of what they expect of each other. It also gives team members licence to challenge each other, if necessary.

Cooperation and collaboration

You can encourage this type of behaviour by asking for ideas, information or support that might help each member with work they are about to undertake. Encourage pairs or small groups to work together on some tasks (although these groups should be changed and rotated throughout the life of the project to avoid cliques developing). Openly share and discuss developments and achievements, as well as problems and how to resolve them. (Getting your team to work collaboratively will be easier if you successfully outlined and openly valued the knowledge, skills and experience each member has, in advance.)

Getting to know you

Make sure this part isn't relegated to formal meetings – people don't get to know each other well when they're dealing with agendas or focused on specific tasks. Hold a pre-meeting before work starts in earnest. Working together also helps as people share opinions and the odd joke across desks or around the water-cooler. Look for opportunities for the team to socialise – perhaps informal gatherings before or after meetings, or social events away from work premises. Don't make these compulsory however, or it could detract from demonstration of personal commitment and engagement.

If you are working with remote teams, make sure you provide members with opportunities to get to know one another. Ideally this should be done in face-to-face meetings or video conferencing at the start of the project. However, you should also encourage other forms of informal contact, such as visiting one another at their places of work or using online chat engines, sharing photos of holidays online etc.

This stage can be missed out where team members feel that they know each other well. However, this approach can undermine team identity as the team may not then stand out from other general work groups. So, make sure you still make time for people to socialise informally, for example asking team members to meet early for coffee, encouraging people to informally discuss how they are feeling about the project, through to what they're doing at the weekend. Again, these sessions should not be mandatory, but instead offer a relaxed, informal environment for the team to be open with one another.

Communication

You can raise the issue of communication with the team at the beginning of the project – what methods of communication do different team members prefer? What level of communication/how much detail is required? How often does the team need to meet to communicate updates to everyone? How can the team ensure the communication is two-way? Debating these points will help the team establish a communication system that works particularly well for them.

Not all communication needs to go through the team leader. This type of control can prevent team members from quickly exchanging ideas and firing off information to colleagues. You should therefore encourage all forms of communication, both formal and informal. Try to ensure that team members don't hoard information, as if it were like the stripes on a police officer's uniform – the more you have, the more powerful you are! This is the main cause of team members' reluctance to share information. The way you behave with information is, therefore, important – share as much as you can with all members, not just some of them. You could also set up systems to help them share information, such as shared drives or places on the intranet where they can upload and download documents for other team members to use.

Encourage team members to communicate in different ways. We tend to interpret information more accurately when it comes in a 'media-rich' format, such as face-to-face and video conferencing. The use of media-rich communication helps generate trust more quickly than 'media poor' forms, like email. This is because we're given more information – not just the message but how the messenger feels about it and other signals including voice or body language. This is especially important for remote teams which meet in person infrequently, if at all.

Empowerment

Empowerment is not about letting people do exactly what they want to without consideration for others. It's about encouraging your team members to bring ideas and discuss options. You need to offer guidance – but accept that it may be disregarded! Real empowerment can be scary, but it's also one of the most effective development techniques for both leaders and members of teams.

Celebrating success

Celebrate successes within the team, for example during team meetings. It's important you let senior colleagues in the organisation know about the team's success, to augment pride and motivation. All too often, celebrating successes is left until the end of the project, whereas it could have prevented loss of momentum or despondency along the way. If you are going to reward the reaching of 'milestones' or other achievements, make sure you involve the whole team. Identifying one or two individuals will only increase competitiveness and, potentially, division in the team. Certainly, acknowledge them openly but make sure the whole team is rewarded to reinforce the message that everyone is working toward the same end.

Commitment

Commitment

Should you find commitment flagging, try to find out why at the earliest opportunity – don't just leave it to sort itself out, because the chances are it won't. Talk to those you think are losing commitment because they will give you the quickest diagnosis of any 'issues'. It may be something pertinent to them and their approach to work; it may be that progress is slow and momentum needs to be increased. It may be that people don't see that you are committed, perhaps because you've cancelled meetings, or appear to pay only cursory attention to developments. Whatever it is, identify it fast, because both commitment and loss of commitment are contagious.

● SUMMARY

Whatever situation you find yourself in when having to create a team, take the time to really consider the important elements involved, as we've described them. It doesn't have to be an arduous process. By factoring in as many parts of the jigsaw as possible you'll have every chance of success. Good luck!

● FURTHER INFORMATION

If you found this tool useful then you are likely to find the following tools both insightful and relevant:

- How to motivate others
- How to raise energy levels
- How to develop rapport
- How to build and maintain trust
- How to engage others to deliver.

● REFERENCES

1 Fitousi, D., & Wenger, M. J. (2011). Processing capacity under perceptual and cognitive load: A closer look at load theory. Journal of Experimental Psychology: Human Perception and Performance, 37(3), 781.

2 Tajfael, H. (1978) (Ed.) Differentiation Between Social Groups: Studies in the Social Psychology of Intergroup Relations. London: Academic Press

3 Simon, B., & Pettigrew, T. F. (2012). Social identity and perceived group homogeneity: Evidence for the ingroup homogeneity effect. European Journal of Social Psychology, 20(4), 269-286.

4 Turner, J. et al (1987). Rediscovering the social group: A self-categorization theory. Oxford: Blackwell.

HOW TO BUILD AND MAINTAIN TRUST

Recognise what trust comprises
and how to increase levels
of trust.

● ISN'T IT INTERESTING?

It is not easy to trust other people. That's not opinion, but fact.

Do you trust me?

We are, according to evolutionary psychologists, hard-wired to detect risk. Over the many hundreds of thousands of years of our evolution, we have maintained some of the core instincts that would have alerted us to threat and danger when roaming the savannah plains. Indeed, we are almost six times more sensitive to threatening stimuli or situations than to 'safe' and non-threatening stimuli. So does this mean that we can spot threats, lies or even frauds easily?

How good are we at knowing who to trust and when to trust them?

Truth is in the eye of the beholder

There are different types of trust present in our everyday relationships. For example, there is emotional trust (do I feel that this person shares my values, principles, beliefs and that they will be on my wavelength?) and cognitive trust (is this person factually credible and do I believe what this person says?).

Our trust mechanisms may not be as strong or as reliable as we think. There has been a lot of research examining the different behaviours between liars and those telling the truth.[1] A key difference is in the language used – and in particular, the level of detail provided when naturally telling the truth.

It seems, not surprisingly, that people don't like elaborating on facts when they are fabricating a story. As a result, those who lie will typically use fewer words and provide less detail in their descriptions. So whilst most of us might typically look into the eyes of another person to determine their trustworthiness, perhaps closing our eyes and listening more carefully might be of more value.

This tool can help

Building trust is often a challenge whether you have a personal relationship with people or not. This tool is about how to build and maintain trust and will help you to recognise what trust comprises and how to increase levels of trust.

● WHY BUILD TRUST?

The level to which we trust those around us is critical to the success or otherwise of our collaboration and relationships with them. Employees who lack trust in one another will spend time – which would otherwise be used more constructively – monitoring one another, duplicating each other's work and generally communicating less effectively. In extreme cases, people will deliberately withhold information or refuse to cooperate altogether.

To prevent these kinds of problems, it's important to build trust at the start of working relationships – but how do you do that when you've never worked with someone before or know nothing about them?

This can be tough because, for most of us, the concept of trust is significant – involving the kind of personal investment we would only make after much trying and testing of someone or something. But, it's easier than that...

First, we'll explain that there are different kinds of trust – three, in fact: 'cognitive', 'transactional' and 'affective'. The first two can be achieved quickly, the third takes longer.

Types of trust[2]

Cognitive trust

This is the first stage or level of trust reached in working relationships. It's easy to achieve quickly amongst people who have no prior knowledge of each other, such as colleagues or clients.

Cognitive trust is about convincing others you have what's required to complete a task with them, including things like knowledge, ability, professionalism, reliability and integrity.

It is, therefore, best described as a 'task based' trust because it's achieved when you convince others of facts about yourself which demonstrate your capability and competence. It can be achieved through communication, even when introducing yourself, by:

- Describing similar, previous projects you have worked on successfully
- Referring to your relevant knowledge and experience
- Specifying your relevant skills and how you have used them before.

So, this is different to the kind of trust built with a long-standing and much loved friend, who, nevertheless, you might not trust to cut your hair or check your car's brakes! In other words, to build cognitive trust you need to establish relevant facts, regardless of whatever else you know or feel about someone.

Cognitive trust is reinforced, on an ongoing basis by:

- Demonstrating your knowledge in discussion
- Using your relevant skills
- Relating your own past experiences to teach others and help them avoid mistakes
- Demonstrating your skills, to prove that they are as you have described them.

Cognitive trust is fragile, however, because it's based on an understanding of skills and experience only. It is easy to damage by, say, missing a deadline or making a mistake in which case the sort of behaviour we mentioned at the start, of colleagues monitoring or duplicating each other's work, becomes more likely.

Transactional trust

Building transactional trust occurs through 'psychological contracting'. The model below shows how this works.[3] It's a process by which individuals in a group, who each have particular roles, tasks or requirements, agree ways of assisting and monitoring each other, and renegotiating ways of working together where necessary. In other words, it's about the ways a group interacts and adapts as individual members' needs arise, to ensure achievement of its overall objectives. In this way, the potential for uncertainty, lack of clarity and mistakes is reduced because the group's members have a 'psychological contract' with each other to accommodate and manage such occurrences.

Informing

Each party informs the others of their needs and what they are prepared to offer.

Negotiating

Each party agrees what they are prepared to do for one another.

Monitoring

Each party agrees to monitor one another to ensure the contract is kept and remains fair.

Renegotiating

Renegotiations occur on an ongoing basis, or if one party decides to exit the relationship.

Affective trust

This type of trust, also known as 'emotional' trust, takes longer to achieve but is key to establishing deeper, longer lasting relationships with others. It requires a greater mutual understanding than is gained by knowledge of each other's abilities or through agreements made with them. The way people establish affective trust is to develop sufficient understanding of each other's emotional and social behaviour as to be able, generally, to predict how they will behave in most situations.

Affective trust requires time spent demonstrating:

- Empathy
- Respect
- Active listening
- Interest in the other party (or parties).

It also depends on the kind of non-verbal behaviour which communicates:

- Warmth
- Attentiveness.

The Trust Ladder

Use the ladder — showing the sorts of behaviour that builds or loses trust — to reflect on how often you behave in ways that both win and lose trust. What do you do well? What opportunities does it reveal for you to improve your trust building skills?

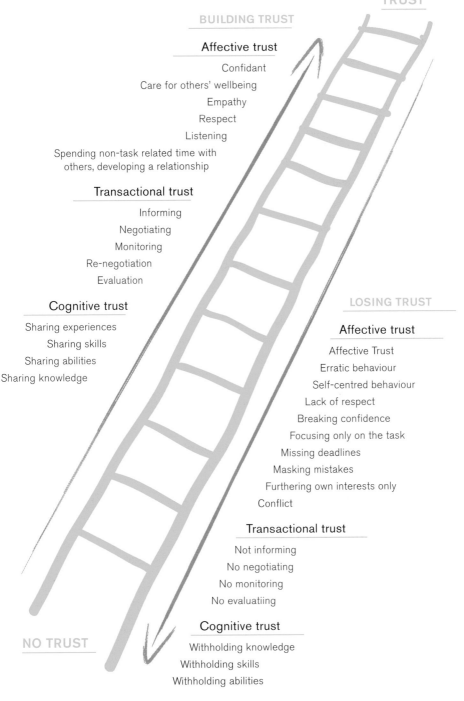

TRUST

BUILDING TRUST

Affective trust
Confidant
Care for others' wellbeing
Empathy
Respect
Listening
Spending non-task related time with
others, developing a relationship

Transactional trust
Informing
Negotiating
Monitoring
Re-negotiation
Evaluation

Cognitive trust
Sharing experiences
Sharing skills
Sharing abilities
Sharing knowledge

LOSING TRUST

Affective trust
Affective Trust
Erratic behaviour
Self-centred behaviour
Lack of respect
Breaking confidence
Focusing only on the task
Missing deadlines
Masking mistakes
Furthering own interests only
Conflict

Transactional trust
Not informing
No negotiating
No monitoring
No evaluatiing

Cognitive trust
Withholding knowledge
Withholding skills
Withholding abilities

NO TRUST

● EMPATHY – WHAT IS IT AND HOW CAN I BUILD IT?

This is the most important requirement of all to building trust at any of the levels described so far and involves both 'perspective taking' and 'empathic concern':[4]

- **'Perspective taking'** involves taking the time to listen to someone else's opinion before making a decision, anticipating their feelings or reactions and considering matters from their point of view, or 'perspective'
- **'Empathic concern'** is the ability to vicariously experience another's reactions and feelings – or 'putting yourself in their shoes.'

Empathy is more than effective listening. It involves setting aside your own feelings and opinions and showing someone else that you understand what they are communicating – as if from within their own experience of it, yet remaining separate. In other words, it's about understanding the person in addition to what he or she is telling you.

Practical steps to achieve empathy[5]

Reflection of feelings and content

To empathise with another, you need to watch and listen for both verbal and non-verbal messages. This means checking that you understand the underlying and often implicit emotions which accompany statements, by verbalising them for the speaker to confirm or otherwise ('reflection of feeling'). For example, if you think they sound anxious, ask whether this is how they are feeling.

'Reflection of content' means repeating statements made to demonstrate your attention and verify mutual understanding.

Other ways to build empathy could include:

- Sharing similar experiences of your own
- 'Mirroring' or copying the other person's behaviour, but in subtle ways, such as sitting if they are seated, or adjusting the speed and tone of your voice
- Showing them that you are trying to see things from their perspective
- Noticing how the other person is feeling as well as what they are saying
- Paraphrasing or summarising what they have told you when they have finished, to check your understanding
- Asking for (and showing that you welcome) feedback.

● ADDITIONAL TIPS FOR BUILDING EMPATHY

Speak up and provide your views

Appearing to not contribute to conversations can lead to misunderstanding and mistrust. So, talk easily and openly – without dominating things. However, if you have an 'issue' to resolve with someone, try not to talk about them behind their backs. It's much better to confront matters dispassionately, in an open and honest way which often creates more positive relationships. In addition, you will, at least, build a reputation for being straightforward rather than as a gossip or trouble-maker. The alternative is to let frustrations fester which can cause irreparable damage.

Authenticity

Does your body language match what you're saying? If not, you're sending confusing messages which will lead people to conclude that you're someone who's 'difficult to read' or 'not what he seems' but this doesn't mean you have to gesticulate wildly to 'act out' what you're saying. For example, if you say you're willing to help a colleague with a presentation next week, but slouch in your chair and roll your eyes at the same time, they're likely to doubt that you mean what you say!

Keep your word

This not only means doing what you said you would. It involves respecting others by keeping confidential information they may have divulged, to yourself.

Invest time in being organised

Manage your time so you can honour commitments you have made. Ask yourself how long it will realistically take you to complete tasks and agree feasible targets with your colleagues and/or manager. If you need to reschedule your time, tell others as soon as possible to not only limit the consequences for them but prevent them forming a negative impression of you.

Do not take advantage/play fair

It's quite normal to build close working relationships at work. Be careful, though, not to use these relationships to gain an advantage over others. Being open and honest about your dealings with your colleagues helps to build trust.

● NEXT STEPS

You should by now have more of a sense of how to build and maintain trust. Here are some suggestions about what to do next:

Discuss delivery style with someone

Talk about how to build and maintain trust with someone who you trust, such as your line manager, mentor, coach or colleague. Think about what you want from this person – do you want a sounding board? Do you want advice and guidance or do you want someone to help review and check your progress?

Look for opportunities to practise

Watch out for opportunities in your current work or elsewhere to practise some of the tips and exercises that you have picked up from this tool.

Evaluate your relationships

Take some time to consider the most important relationships that you currently have and the level of trust that you feel exists. Consider one or two people who you would like to feel more trust between you and them. For each person think about what you can work on to build more trust. Use this reflection to help you to build trust with new people.

● FURTHER INFORMATION

If you found this tool useful, then you are likely to find the following tools both insightful and relevant:

- How to influence others
- How to develop rapport
- How to manage your impact
- How to create team identity
- How to give feedback.

● REFERENCES

1   Littlepage, G. & Pineault, T. (1978). Verbal, Facial, and Paralinguistic Cues to the Detection of Truth and Lying. **Personality and Social Psychology Bulletin,** 4(3), 461-464.

2   Kanawattanachai, P. & Youngjin, Y. (2005). Dynamic Nature of Trust in Virtual Teams, **Sprouts: Working Papers on Information Environments, Systems and Organizations,** 2(2), 41–58.

3   Herriot, P. & Pemberton, C. (1997). Facilitating New Deals. **Human Resource Management Journal,** 7, 45–56.

4   Murgatroyd, S. (1985). **Psychology in Action: Counselling and Helping.** London. British Psychological Society and Methuen.

5   Hayes, J. (1991). **Interpersonal skills: Goal Directed behaviour at work.** London. Harper Collins.

HOW TO GAIN BUY-IN AND COMMITMENT

Understand how to influence and persuade even the most cynical people around you and recognise the factors that can help you gain commitment from those you work with.

● ISN'T IT INTERESTING?

What do you need to survive?

What motivates those around you?

Identifying what makes others tick will inform you of how best to gain their buy-in and commitment. Researchers have studied in great detail how and why people make commitments, and to what ends they make those commitments.

A hierarchy of needs

In 1971, Abraham Maslow[1] proposed the theory that we are driven by a hierarchy of needs and that humans strive for the highest level of personal attainment (the highest being called 'self-actualisation'). This theory is still used now, and a modern study in Israel[2] showed a correlation between self-actualisation and a positive attitude towards, and success in finding, employment.

Maslow developed a hierarchy with five levels of basic needs, based on the notion that individuals progress through the levels but will not progress to the next level until the needs of the first have been satisfied, and so on. These needs are:

- Physiological – where we initially seek to satisfy needs or things (like food and shelter).

- Safety – at work this includes physical safety (such as clothing that is protective, protection against unemployment or loss of income through sickness).

- Social – includes the need to belong (at work this could be through working alongside colleagues who are supportive, communicative and team-orientated).

- Esteem – includes being given recognition for a job well done, as many seek the esteem and respect of others. Promotion at work might achieve this.

- Self-actualisation – (the need to realise one's full potential) – this is often measured by the extent of success and/or challenge at work.

This tool can help

Everyone is motivated in different ways. This fact impacts on how we get others on board and how we can develop commitment in those we work alongside. This tool is about how to gain buy-in and commitment and will assist you in understanding how to influence and persuade even the most cynical people around you and to recognise the factors that can help you gain commitment from those you work with.

● 7-STEP BUY-IN MODEL

People aren't always going to jump on the bandwagon with your ideas; sometimes they need a little persuasion. Getting people to invest resources (their time, their budget, department, etc.) in your plans over anyone else's seems like a daunting task, but anybody can do it.

It's not easy to persuade numerous, very different people – each with their own priorities and agendas – to commit or 'buy-in' to a new initiative or project. Some people seem to have a knack for it – but rather than being to do with an innate 'winning' personality, it's more often to do with following an effective plan. Here's one that you can use yourself:

You need to make a 7-stage plan – this is our model of it:

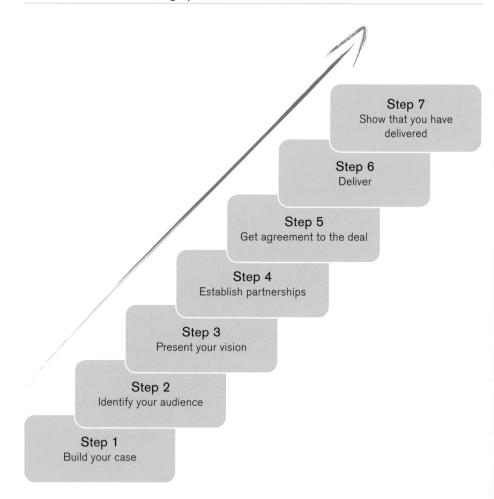

Step 7
Show that you have delivered

Step 6
Deliver

Step 5
Get agreement to the deal

Step 4
Establish partnerships

Step 3
Present your vision

Step 2
Identify your audience

Step 1
Build your case

A STEP-BY-STEP GUIDE TO GAINING BUY-IN

Step 1: Build your case

Once you have your idea, consider how it might translate in reality. Gather facts and information to both support it and demonstrate that you have researched staff surveys, company policies or spoken to others in the organisation to establish how it would 'fit' or bring measurable benefit. Just theorising and second guessing will only get you tied in knots at the first detailed analysis by someone else.

We will deal with how to build your case and win commitment from potential stakeholders in a later section. For now you need to think about how you will create a solid foundation for your idea.

Step 2: Identify your audience

Think about these questions to establish whether you've identified the right people to talk to:

- Why is it necessary to gain commitment from this stakeholder?
- What benefit will their commitment bring?

Remember, you may have many stakeholders, each with different agendas. Identifying your target audience will help you to pitch your idea at the right level, capture their interest, gain their understanding and achieve buy-in.

Those with decision making authority may have different concerns and priorities. Taking the time to find out what these are will help you present your idea in a way which captures their interest and therefore is more likely to win their commitment. Try to anticipate the kind of questions you'll be asked by those with different roles and perspectives. You could also bolster the idea's feasibility by suggesting support from tried and tested external sources, which may help to ease any concerns about possible associated risks.

Step 3: Present your vision

People think in stories and narratives more than facts and figures. A large part of being a great orator and gaining buy-in is being able to weave an engaging vision for the future outcome of this activity. Leadership effectiveness has been found to have strong correlations with the ability to present a clear and inspirational vision to subordinate workers.[3]

Further information on presenting your vision is given in a later section.

Step 4: Establish partnerships

Identify the tasks you need to delegate and to whom, to sustain progress. Be flexible about how they might fit these tasks in amongst their existing responsibilities and explain the benefits to them of contributing to the project.

Step 5: Get agreement to the deal

If yours is a long-term project, present it as a series of recognisable, achievable stages and agree a practical timescale for each with the appropriate decision makers. Referring to decisions you already have agreement for will help secure others and, as you proceed, this will make it easier to increase buy-in to the overall project and boost momentum generally.

Step 6: Deliver

Making sure each stage of the project happens on time will be easier if you've followed the advice above, and established who is responsible for different contributions. If things seem to be working according to plan and on time it will maintain people's interest and commitment.

Step 7: Show them that you have delivered

Once committed, stakeholders will want to know about the rewards and benefits of investing their reputation, time or other resources. Closely monitor all effort and achievement at every stage of the project and make sure you communicate benefits to the business as a whole. If there were people who expressed doubt or misgivings at the start, this will help win them over, too!

● BUILDING YOUR CASE

Organise your case! Collect evidence to support your idea and check the following:

Get the facts right

The business reasons

The ethical approach

The legal standpoint

Your Unique Selling Points (USPs)

The confident sell – because this is just the best!

Get the facts right

Try to establish as much information and background data as possible, not just about your own idea but possible alternatives too. Consider both the benefits and risks.

The business reasons

Make it clear how your idea aligns with or promotes the business's goals and objectives.

The ethical approach

Show that your idea accords with best practice by demonstrating its integrity and that it won't compromise the business's reputation or working partnerships.

The legal standpoint

Check whether the law or internal policies and practices support or hinder any of your arguments.

Your Unique Selling Points (USPs)

What's different about your idea? Find a way to express its unique logic or creativity to capture and 'hook' your audience's interest and imagination.

The confident sell

If you've looked at all the angles and you genuinely believe in the plan you're putting forward, people will notice this confidence and it will in turn inspire confidence in them.

● PRESENTING YOUR VISION

Top tips to presenting your vision:

1. Tailor your approach by emphasising those aspects of your idea to which the majority of your audience will react positively.

2. Outline the key facts simply. Leave the detail to later. What is your idea? What are its most important elements? How will it work?

3. Highlight both pros and cons and make it clear you've given thought to reducing potential risks.

4. Generate enthusiasm for your idea by explaining why it's necessary and the benefits it will deliver, with energy and conviction.

5. Start and finish on a high because research shows that audiences are likely to remember the first and last part of any communication more readily.

6. Consider the broader implications of your idea in the context of what the business is trying to achieve and indicate how it would contribute to future success.

● GAIN BUY-IN PREFERENCE TEST

We've designed this exercise to help you establish the best methods to use, according to your personality, to achieve buy-in. It will help you persuade others to commit to your idea when presenting your views and establish partnerships and winning agreements to the 'deal' (stages 3-5 of our model). Complete the questionnaire below to identify the methods you'd choose and then use the 'preferences table' (starting on page 99) to understand more about them.

There are 16 items, each describing a specific approach to gaining 'buy-in'. Using the scale below, rate how often you demonstrate each one described. Circle the score in the corresponding 'Self Assessment' column overpage.

1 = Almost never demonstrated

2

3 = Occasionally demonstrated

4

5 = Sometimes demonstrated

6

7 = Frequently demonstrated

8

9 = Almost always demonstrated

Item	Self Assessment								
1. You are influential and persuasive in the way you put your point across.	1	2	3	4	5	6	7	8	9
2. You put across the key pieces of data that make your idea worthwhile.	1	2	3	4	5	6	7	8	9
3. You place the emphasis on the opportunities that your idea will bring.	1	2	3	4	5	6	7	8	9
4. You demonstrate high levels of persistence in the face of obstacles and challenges.	1	2	3	4	5	6	7	8	9
5. You are energetic and enthusiastic when sharing your own vision of what can be achieved.	1	2	3	4	5	6	7	8	9
6. You use logic and high-level analysis to cut through complexity for a clear solution.	1	2	3	4	5	6	7	8	9
7. You underline the unique selling points of your idea.	1	2	3	4	5	6	7	8	9
8. You understand the points on which you are prepared to compromise.	1	2	3	4	5	6	7	8	9
9. You tailor your idea to meet the needs of the audience.	1	2	3	4	5	6	7	8	9
10. You outline the idea in a logical order.	1	2	3	4	5	6	7	8	9
11. You point out the innovative aspects of your idea.	1	2	3	4	5	6	7	8	9
12. You actively seek to promote your ideas.	1	2	3	4	5	6	7	8	9
13. You adapt your approach according to different people's agendas.	1	2	3	4	5	6	7	8	9
14. You outline the pros and cons of your idea.	1	2	3	4	5	6	7	8	9
15. You highlight the ways in which your idea is better than alternatives.	1	2	3	4	5	6	7	8	9
16. You ensure that you gain some kind of commitment when you have proposed your idea.	1	2	3	4	5	6	7	8	9

● SCORING

Add up each 'area' score, on this table:

Area	Item to Add	Total Score
The art of persuasion	1 + 5 + 9 + 13	
Logical fact	2 + 6 + 10 + 14	
Sell the benefits	3 + 7 + 11 + 15	
Negotiate the deal	4 + 8 + 12 + 16	

The higher the score, out of a possible 36 for each 'area', the more you'll tend to rely on it. You're likely to use one as your primary method, but most of us will also use the other methods as a secondary measure to mix things up. The pie chart shows the prevalence of methods in a hypothetical individual who has taken the test.

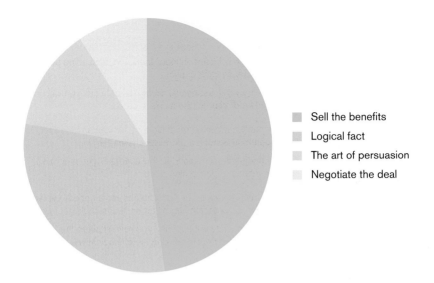

- Sell the benefits
- Logical fact
- The art of persuasion
- Negotiate the deal

● WHAT THIS MEANS FOR YOU

Primary Preference	Secondary Preference	
The art of persuasion	Logical facts	You mostly rely on using logic to influence and persuade people. It makes sense to you and you present the key points to win their commitment. Risk: Be careful not to oversell the positive aspects and downplay the risks. You may only target people who respond to facts and figures and neglect describing the overall concept.
	Sell the benefits	You tend to rely most on your presentation style. You're likely to use energy and enthusiasm to try to sell the positive aspects to stakeholders. Risk: Be careful not to oversell the positive aspects and downplay the risks. You may try to target those who will respond to the concept rather than hard facts and figures.
	Negotiate the deal	You're probably aware of your ability to influence others and use this to try to persuade them of a 'best case' outcome. Risk: You may have a tendency to be very persuasive about your plan's immediate benefits but fail to describe what it may deliver in the long-term or in a broader context.

Primary Preference	Secondary Preference	
Logical facts	The art of persuasion	Your approach is based on logic, facts and persuading people to 'see the sense' of your plan. **Risk:** You may rely too heavily on factual data and you will need to be certain of your information's accuracy.
	Sell the benefits	You probably outline the rationale for your idea and then focus on its potential benefits to forestall challenges. **Risk:** If people don't respond to this approach, you may lack another means of persuading them.
	Negotiate the deal	You may simply present the facts, figures and a general explanation – then open a discussion about how someone could get involved. **Risk:** Your idea may not appeal if you haven't taken the time to describe and 'sell' the overall idea more imaginatively.

Primary Preference	Secondary Preference	
Sell the benefits	The art of persuasion	You tend to rely on emphasising the opportunities your idea offers to persuade people to commit to it. **Risk:** You might be challenged about the plan's detail and your logic.
	Logical facts	You primarily focus on the benefits of your idea, supported by key facts and figures. **Risk:** If this approach doesn't work first time, you may struggle to negotiate commitment.
	Negotiate the deal	You probably outline your plan's real or potential benefits, then ask how or when people can schedule their contribution. **Risk:** Some people may not be persuaded without a detailed explanation of your rationale or your plan's broader relevance.

Primary Preference	Secondary Preference	
Negotiate the deal	The art of persuasion	You're likely to concentrate on getting some kind of commitment and probably use different methods to do so. **Risk:** You may risk alienating people with this approach by appearing to 'steamroller' them, especially if they need time to reflect and consider.
	Logical facts	You're likely to rely on presenting the facts about how your idea would work, then push for agreement on that basis alone. **Risk:** You may not appeal to people who respond to a more intuitive, empathetic or imaginative approach.
	Sell the benefits	You tend to outline the benefits and unique selling points of your proposition – then push for a deal. **Risk:** You may risk demonstrating limited consideration for potential risks as well as the more positive aspects.

● NEXT STEPS

Use the table below to think about the approach you'd use to persuade people to commit. Then, consider how you could build on this approach or develop and use other methods to increase your effectiveness.

Primary Preference:
Secondary Preference:

How can I build on my approach?

How can I develop the other areas of gaining commitment?

What opportunities do I have or will I have in the future?

● FURTHER INFORMATION

If you found this tool useful, then you are likely to find the following tools both insightful and relevant:

- How to be assertive
- How to influence others
- How to develop rapport
- How to communicate effectively
- How to actively listen
- How to manage your impact
- How to build and maintain trust
- How to make reasoned judgements
- How to win and manage resources.

● REFERENCES

1   Maslow, A.H. (1971). **The farther reaches of human nature.** New York: Penguin Compass

2   Huss, E., & Magos, M. (2012). Relationship between self-actualisation and employment for at-risk young unemployed women. **Journal of Education and Work,** (ahead-of-print), 1-17.

3   Berson, Y., Shamir, B., Avolio, B. J., & Popper, M. (2001). The relationship between vision strength, leadership style, and context. **The Leadership Quarterly,** 12(1), 53-73.

HOW TO SUPPORT AND CHALLENGE IN TANDEM

Understand the interplay between support and challenge, establish the right balance between these two and recognise implications for the effective performance of your staff.

● ISN'T IT INTERESTING?

What makes us want to get out there and make a difference? Take these people... what do they need to make them dynamic and go-getting rather than bored and uninterested?

Knowing when to support and when to challenge

How do you manage staff so that they perform to the best of their abilities? Effective motivation depends on many factors such as pay, job structure and work conditions. One factor that seems to outweigh all others, however, is the degree to which you can positively affect people's levels of attention and interest in what they're doing, as demonstrated in the following research into behaviour at work.

Are you paying attention?

Several years back, researchers conducted a study into whether paying attention or 'mindfulness' had a positive impact on stress and health behaviours.[1] Hundreds of undergraduates were studied on their behaviours regarding paying attention, their stress levels and their adherence to health-related behaviours such as eating fruit & vegetables, and exercise.

Those who had a tendency to 'drift off' and paid less attention during their everyday lives were surprisingly found to be more stressed overall. Additionally, those who were more mindful were more likely to engage in healthy behaviours and have a more positive outlook.

It just shows that if you're feeling like your mind wants to drift off during a meeting or when doing the chores, keep with it, it's good for you!

This tool can help

Getting people to pay attention is just one of the good possible outcomes of successfully supporting and challenging. However, it is important to interplay these two tactics, so you are not making yourself obstructive, or a push-over. This tool is designed to help you get this balance right and make the most out of your leadership by directing and motivating your employees.

● WHAT IS MEANT BY CHALLENGE AND SUPPORT?

Challenge

Many people think challenge is something negative. Talking about 'challenging others' in most discussions about personal or professional development is often assumed to mean disagreeing with others in some way. The word 'challenge', in fact, has three different definitions.

1: a demanding or stimulating situation.
2: a call to engage in contest, fight, or argument.
3: a questioning of a statement or fact.

This isn't all negative – indeed, the first definition can be extremely positive. Challenging will of course sometimes mean ruffling some feathers, but that doesn't mean it can't have a decent outcome. What most senior leaders would regard as a successful challenge is where an employee needs to take a different approach in their actions, and you successfully negotiate them onto this path. There are several ways to do this depending on the situation; for more information look at the 'How to influence others' iLEAD™ tool.

Support

When we talk about support in the workplace we mean providing some form of assistance to others. Again, a dictionary definition may be useful:

1: to give practical or emotional help to someone.
2: to give approval to (a cause, political idea).
3: to take an active interest in and be loyal…

Again, different circumstances require different means of support. Understanding what kind of support is required in a situation is vital to providing the necessary help and encouragement.

So, when challenging people, it may be necessary to offer support at the same time to provide the necessary balance of reinforcement. For example, if you found something at work very challenging you might find it useful to have someone to talk to about it. Supporting and challenging others requires flexibility according to their differing requirements – and getting this balance right is where you can make the biggest difference to performance, commitment and motivation.

● MOTIVATIONAL WELLBEING

Prof. Cary Cooper and his colleague Prof. Ivan Robertson have conducted decades of research into workplace psychology, including motivational factors. Clearly, you want motivated people at work because without motivation, people may not perform or may become disengaged and eventually look for work elsewhere. Below is a Robertson-Cooper[2] model showing the relationship between pressure (challenge) and performance.

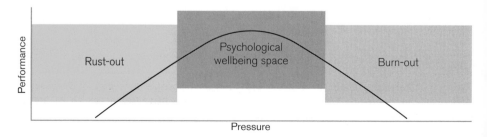

If there is not enough pressure on people, they are likely to 'rust out' and this can be just as stressful as too much pressure. However, under too much pressure people are likely to 'burn out'. From a wellbeing perspective, in order to enable people to perform at their best, you need to get the level of pressure right, which importantly includes the level of challenge offered.

Now look at this again, but in conjunction with support. This involves getting the best out of ourselves and others and relies on the right balance of support and challenge. This means providing encouragement and recognition whilst being prepared to point out discrepancies and ask questions.

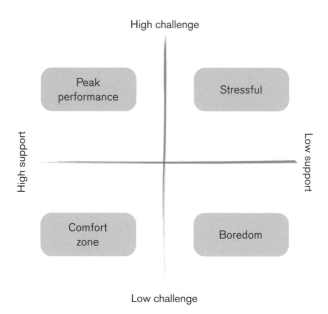

This is another model by Robertson-Cooper[3] which illustrates that if you apply pressure and challenge people, provided you give them support at the same time, the result can be peak performance. Without support, the result is stress. If, therefore, you challenge somebody beyond their comfort zone, whether in a developmental or performance context, adequate support is needed to achieve success.

One of the key things is to establish as a manager how much support you provide. People are not dramatically different from one another, but if their preferences for low or high support are not recognised they may 'burn out' from being over challenged or 'rust out' through being over supported. Both diagrams show the importance of support and challenge to get employees into a position of peak performance.

● STRENGTHS AND RISKS

The table overleaf will give you a chance to think back on some situations where you needed to challenge and/or support at work. Firstly, you will need to think of some situations in the past where a colleague was engaging in non-ideal behaviour and you felt that you needed to intervene (regardless of whether you did or didn't).

Once you have thought of a few examples, you can use your own experiences of the situation, and what you've learned from this tool to put down what, if any, challenge and support is needed. We've provided one hypothetical example to get you started.

Situation that needs resolving	Possible ways to support	Possible ways to challenge
A new intern is consistently failing to meet deadlines You are their line manager	Offer some coaching to improve his/her efficiency Ask for colleagues to hand down more reasonable deadlines	Challenge the intern about whether they are spending too much time on their phone/Facebook Challenge their tendency to turn up late for work

● GETTING THE BALANCE RIGHT

So, how do you challenge and support at the same time?

There are a number of factors which are vital to achieving this most difficult of balancing acts:

- **Acknowledge the person**
  When considering what someone is telling or asking you, it is important to show recognition of the points they are making or the situation they describe.

- **Ask and listen**
  Entering into a dialogue by asking questions and listening to replies helps to build knowledge and gain an understanding of the situation.

- **Describe the situation**
  It is often useful to outline the situation to somebody or ask them to elaborate on their perspective. This helps build a picture of what is happening in order to gauge the right amount of support or challenge required.

- Explore the implications
  Investigating the wider effects or implications of an issue can help raise awareness of its overall impact.

- Recognise feelings
  Recognising the possible emotional aspect of a situation may take the dialogue to a different level. It may not otherwise be immediately apparent that emotional support is required.

- Make a clear statement
  Making your expectation absolutely clear ensures that there is no ambiguity.

Consider how this model is used to good effect in the following example of feedback:

Acknowledging

the other person's position:

'I can see you feel you have been unfairly treated'

ASKING the other person's views and LISTENING and accepting that this is how they see it, even if you disagree with what they say:

'How do you see…?' 'Do you agree with…?'

Describing

factually, the specific situation you are unhappy about:

'You have been delivering the reports two or three weeks late, for four months, and…'

Effects

describing factually the effects of the actions with which you are dissatisfied:

'…and the effects are that the budget figures are two or three weeks late, which means that…'

Feelings

stating your feelings, reactions and opinions resulting from the other person's actions:

'I get annoyed when…' 'I'm not satisfied with…'

Provide A CLEAR STATEMENT of what you want to change and how:

'What I want is….'

Summary

It is important to get the balance right between support and challenge in order to help others grow and improve. Remember that to challenge someone is not necessarily negative but can be about pushing them to improve or change. Coupled with the right type of support it can make the difference between boredom or stress and peak performance.

● FURTHER INFORMATION

If you found this tool useful, then you are likely to find the following tools both insightful and relevant:

- How to be assertive
- How to manage your impact
- How to manage difficult conversations
- How to develop others
- How to challenge others effectively
- How to engage others to deliver.

● REFERENCES

1 Roberts, K. C., & Danoff-Burg, S. (2010). Mindfulness and health behaviors: is paying attention good for you?. Journal of American College Health, 59(3), 165-173.

2 Robertson, I. T., Cooper, G. L., & Williams, J. (1990). The validity of the Occupational Stress Indicator. Work & Stress, 4: 29-39.

3 J. Arnold, I.T. Robertson and C.L. Cooper (1991). Work psychology: Understanding human behaviour in the workplace, United Kingdom: Longman.

HOW TO GIVE FEEDBACK

Give constructive feedback and recognise the potential responses in order to pitch your message at the appropriate level.

● ISN'T IT INTERESTING?

Can you believe what fortune tellers tell you?

Do you trust me?

Many people are interested in the 'insights' that fortune tellers, astrologers and palm readers claim to give. However, in the absence of real information, many of their techniques rely on 'subjective validation'; a bias in our thinking where we find personal or significant meaning in the information presented. Combine this with our selective nature about what we pay attention to – accepting the information that confirms what we think about ourselves and rejecting information that contradicts it – it's easy to see why they are still so popular.

Something we can all relate to...

In 1948, psychologist Bertram R Forer gave a personality test to his students and then gave them a personality analysis based on the test's results.[1] Each student was asked to rate the analysis for accuracy ('5' being excellent and '0' being very poor). The students were very impressed with the personality tests and scored an average rating of 4.26. Forer then revealed that each student had been given the same analysis; a generic set of words that couldn't possibly have been accurate for everyone. The reason for this is that we can often not scrutinise feedback for its validity if it is vague but appears pleasing at face value. This can ultimately undo the practical intention of feedback, and is counter-productive in many instances.

More recently, a 2012 study[2] into students' coursework feedback found that there was a difference in the level of critical feedback given to minority students. The cause of this was found to be that the predominantly white markers had been hesitant to provide critical feedback for fear of being racist. This is a crucial message to remember with feedback, staying objective and being aware of possible biases; even if you think they are having a positive impact, they can be having the very opposite effect, and negatively impacting on the individual be they a student, or an underperforming employee.

Both of these studies show that while being honest and effective at delivering feedback might seem straightforward, there are still basic steps which can be missed out.

This tool can help

Giving feedback to people helps to provide honest, constructive advice. It is important that the recipient engages with the feedback for the right reasons; thus basing claims on actual behavioural evidence is essential. This tool is about how to give feedback and will help you to give constructive feedback and recognise the potential responses in order to pitch your message at the appropriate level.

● INTRODUCTION: GIVING FEEDBACK AND RECOGNITION

What is feedback and recognition?

Giving feedback and recognition is about sharing your observations of someone with them to enable their self-awareness to grow. This can include giving informal feedback as a means of providing encouragement or addressing a specific incident that has occurred. It can also be in a more formal review or performance appraisal scenario. If feedback is to help people develop themselves and their performance, then it needs to be done in a way that gives them the confidence to make positive changes.

Why is this important?

It is important for your team's development, job satisfaction and, ultimately, performance. Feedback increases self-awareness and, primarily, confirms knowledge about where personal strengths and weaknesses lie. When feedback is used to clarify expectations about work performance it can lead to increased motivation, which then goes on to boost engagement and output. Recognising good work is part and parcel of giving feedback and is one of the main factors contributing to happiness at work. Research shows that positive emotions lead to increased productivity, creativity and discretionary effort (effort beyond the call of duty).

When should you give feedback?

Informal feedback on a regular basis will lead to an open culture where learning is encouraged. In the case of giving feedback about a specific incident, it is important that it is timely and not too long after the event for maximum impact.

Formal feedback on performance should be scheduled on a regular basis that suits both the feedback giver and receiver.

Who will benefit from feedback?

Those who you manage, those who you work alongside and those who manage you will all benefit from different forms of feedback.

How do you give feedback?

This short guide to giving feedback will show you how to:

- Apply the model of Two-Way Feedback and Recognition
- Use an 'appreciative inquiry'
- Give feedback to different kinds of people.

● AN APPRECIATIVE APPROACH TO FEEDBACK

When people know what their strengths are and are able to put them into practice regularly, they are more likely to flourish than when they focus on marginally improving in those areas where they need to develop.

Of course, development areas can be major liabilities and do need to be addressed. People's strengths, however, are often the places where it is possible to see the most significant personal and professional growth.

This appreciative inquiry model of giving feedback is used to take the strengths of an organisation or individual by recognising them, and through a process of evaluation, use these strengths to improve performance.

The appreciative inquiry model[3]

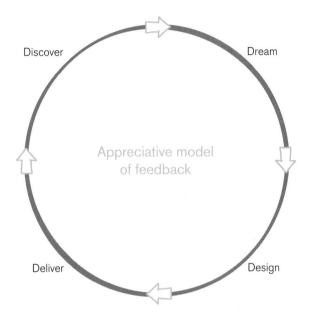

Discover

- Ask the individual to consider what they are like when performing at their best.
- Give examples of occasions when you have observed excellent performance. Be specific about what it was that differentiated the individual from an average performer.
- Explore these incidences and examples and consider how they demonstrate the individual's unique strengths.

Dream

- Ask the individual to consider an area of their work in which they would like to improve – where they are either underperforming or just performing to a satisfactory level.
- Ask them to think of a broad, ideal goal which they would like to move towards, for example 'I would like to get a promotion'.
- Ask the individual to visualise what they would be like if they applied their strengths to the chosen area.

Design

- Explore what the individual would need to do in order to use more of their strengths in the chosen area of work. For example, rely more on building personal relationships to increase sales, use the same creativity that is used for design projects to solve 'people problems', etc.
- Explore whether there are ways that the individual's job needs to develop in order to use more of their strengths; for example, delegating more administrative work to allow time for more project management, or taking on a role in a team project for an afternoon a week.

Deliver

- Together, work out a list of actions necessary to ensure the ideas you have generated are put into practice – make these Specific, Measurable, Achievable, Realistic and Time-limited (SMART).
- Agree what you will need to do to support the individual to achieve their actions.
- Agree on how you will monitor progress.

● SBI MODEL

The SBI model could help you to structure your feedback and help you plan for success when delivering it. SBI stands for 'Structure', 'Behaviour' and 'Impact', explained in more detail below.

Structure

Make sure that you have made clear what the feedback is about and how you intend to present it.

Example Actions: Make clear which situation you are referring to when providing feedback, e.g. 'yesterday you were late to a meeting'. Provide objective evidence which can be examined: 'you entered at 10.15am rather than the scheduled 10.00am'.

Think about how you're going to introduce the issues, and what points you are going to mention, and in which order.

Behaviour

Be aware of and receptive to the participant's behaviour, reactions and body language.

Example Actions: Observe and be open about the person's reactions, e.g. 'you seem disgruntled about what I've told you?'

Don't make assumptions about how a participant will react, and don't make assumptions about why they react the way they do.

Impact

Impress upon the participant the effect that their current behaviour is having, and the impact change could bring.

Example Actions: Inform the participant of comments that have been made by other stakeholders: 'the client said you were late delivering'.

Ask the participant to think from others' perspective about their behaviour: 'do you think that Accounts would believe that you have been fully cooperative with them?'

● GIVING FEEDBACK TO DIFFERENT KINDS OF PEOPLE

We all react differently to feedback. If you don't consider the reaction you are likely to get from someone when you give them feedback there is a chance that your message will not be heard.

Almost certainly, the following feedback personalities are working in your organisation. Before tackling a difficult issue with someone, think about which description fits them the best and let it guide your approach. Be aware though that these are just helpful metaphors; people will not fit perfectly into one category.

The Sponge

The Sponge is both open and receptive to feedback and will actively encourage others to critique their approach. They show a high desire for feedback on their performance.

You will need to make sure that a feedback session with this individual allows time for two-way dialogue, plenty of exploration and translating thoughts into action. To make sure that this individual's need for feedback is met, plan for sessions at regular intervals. Be aware that behind the 'perfect learner' exterior, the Sponge may be seeking reassurance to boost an underlying lack of confidence.

Risk – a constant desire for feedback may devalue important messages.

The Glass Half Empty

The Glass Half Empty has a tendency to focus in on negative feedback, magnify it and overly worry that it may lead to disaster – they will see a small personal flaw as being 'the end of the world'.

To get the best out of a discussion you will need to help this individual put the feedback into perspective and look for ways that they can build on their strengths to overcome their weaknesses. You could help them check their perspective by asking questions like 'what's the worst thing that could happen?' and 'is this always the case or only in some situations?'

Risk – the pessimist will only hear the bad, not the good, messages.

The Bucket

The Bucket appears open to feedback but will not pick up on messages, either positive or negative, unless they are given loudly and clearly.

This individual has a tendency to minimise negative messages so it is important that you check and recheck that your message has been heard. You may need to give the same message a number of times and in different ways.

Risk – subtle feedback will not be picked up on.

The Funnel

The Funnel appears to be accepting of feedback and is, to a certain extent, but is also good at giving the impression of listening without truly doing so.

In a feedback session you will need to frequently ask this individual to reflect back what they have heard, e.g. 'what do you see the most significant points that we have discussed being?' At the end, ask them to take away specific actions. In the longer term, you will need to give practical support and encouragement to ensure that this individual takes the action that they willingly agreed to take.

Risk – the funnel will look willing but do nothing.

The Teacup

The Teacup is highly sensitive to criticism and will be concerned that negative feedback is linked to personal failure.

You will need to give developmental messages using careful diplomatic language and cushion them with appreciation of other strengths and positive messages. This individual needs to feel safe, appreciated and valued before they will be able to learn and grow from developmental feedback. Don't overreact to a teacup's tears as they are a part of this individual's self expression and are usually useful – although be wary if they are used to deflect the feedback!

Risk – they may be crushed and overwhelmed.

The Bullet Proof Vest

The Bullet Proof Vest finds it difficult to see feedback as anything other than ammunition. When you wish to give them feedback they will feel under attack, be defensive and ready to challenge what you say.

You will need to address this defensiveness before giving the feedback and this may mean letting the individual know that they seem defensive, asking them why and persuading them to to explore this with you. You can make it easier for them by letting them know that it is okay for them to challenge, as long as they're willing to be open-minded.

Risk – they won't listen and the relationship will be damaged.

The Stagnant Pond

The Stagnant Pond has heard it all before. They know what their strengths, weaknesses, development areas, favourite competencies and skills are. The trouble with this individual is that they see no reason why they should change themselves – improve their weaknesses or build on their strengths.

As this individual is already fairly self aware and can predict the developmental feedback that you are going to give them, you will need to explore why they have continued receiving the same messages. You may motivate this individual by helping them see how it is within their control to make changes. An appreciative approach will help them visualise their future career and focus on developing in areas that are critical to success.

Risk – a lack of motivation to act will prevent success.

● A MODEL OF TWO-WAY FEEDBACK & RECOGNITION

Giving feedback and recognition to employees works best when it is a two-way process, relying on building clarity, dialogue, exploration and action. There are two people involved, with potentially different objectives and different personal needs. To give feedback that helps the receiver to grow and take action, you will need to consider their objectives as well as your own. You can do this by 'putting yourself into their shoes' and, in the case of giving formal feedback, discussing the objectives of the meeting before you begin.

Clarity

Dialogue

Exploration

Action

The Feedback Giver

Objectives in feedback session:

- To build the employee's self-awareness
- To give clear messages about good and poor performance
- To make sure that poor performance will improve and good performance continues
- To discover the root of any issues.

Personal needs:

- To be given the opportunity for dialogue
- To be a competent/nurturing/successful manager
- To be able to deliver important messages sensitively and have this heard.

The Feedback Receiver

Objectives in feedback session:

- To understand any messages
- To explore positive feedback and justify negative feedback
- To find out if feedback is general or about individual events
- To find out how to develop
- To have the chance to explain personal circumstances.

Personal needs:

- To be heard
- To feel safe
- To feel valued and appreciated
- To have an emotional outlet
- To put feedback into perspective.

Useful tips for giving two-way feedback and recognition

- When appropriate, talk about the meeting's objectives beforehand and aim to create a safe space that will allow openness and honesty.

- To make sure that your conversation is two-way, aim to speak for 30% of the meeting only – spend the rest of the time allowing the employee to reflect and voice their own opinions.

- Focus on positives and what is working before exploring areas of underperformance.

- Keep messages simple and clear, and focus on specific examples rather than general impressions and hearsay.

- Focus on understanding the individual's perception of the situation rather than giving your own.

- It is important to agree actions through discussion rather than gain compliance by being too directive.

- Adapt your feedback style to the type of person you are with – is the person a Sponge, a Teacup, a Bucket or a Funnel? (See section on giving feedback to different kinds of people).

● NEXT STEPS

If you remember three things, make them the following:

1. Feedback is a two-way process and works best when the personal needs and objectives of the feedback giver and receiver are both met.

2. An appreciative approach to feedback will enable you to get the most from your employees.

3. You will need to flex your feedback style depending on the needs of the individuals you are giving feedback to.

Next time you are giving feedback, whether in a performance review meeting or after watching someone in a meeting, take these three points into account and watch the results!

● FURTHER INFORMATION

If you found this tool useful then you are likely to find the following tools both insightful and relevant:

- How to be assertive
- How to influence others
- How to communicate effectively
- How to actively listen
- How to manage difficult conversations
- How to support and challenge in tandem
- How to develop others.

● REFERENCES

1 Forer, B. (1949). The fallacy of personal validation: A classroom demonstration of gullibility. **Journal of Abnormal and Social Psychology,** 44, 118-123.

2 Croft, A., & Schmader, T. (2012). The feedback withholding bias: Minority students do not receive critical feedback from evaluators concerned about appearing racist. **Journal of Experimental Social Psychology.**

3 Cooperrider, D. L., & Whitney, D. (2001). A positive revolution in change: Appreciative inquiry. **Public Administration and Public Policy,** 87, 611-630.

IDENTIFYING PERSONAL MEANING

HOW TO IDENTIFY YOUR PERSONAL MEANING

Be aware of the importance of your core values and personal preferences. Knowledge of these core concepts can help you to understand what you want from your work and how to go about getting it.

● ISN'T IT INTERESTING?

Pepsi – Coca-Cola. Can you tell the difference? Which would you drink and why?

Purpose and direction

Both drinks are marketed at our values and lifestyle rather than on taste. Advertising (such as for these drinks), is full of consumer-focused messages, and it can be hard for us to filter out all the noise and come to an informed conclusion about what we really want.

The Pepsi Challenge

In 2008, Michael Allen and his colleagues[1] at the University of Adelaide set out to test how our values affect our perceptions. They gave participants either Pepsi or a store-brand cola to drink. However, they lied to some of the participants about which drink they had been given in order to see if their values would bias their perception.

Those who most strongly agreed that life should be full of excitement thought that their cola – which they were told was Pepsi – was tastier, whether or not they were actually drinking Pepsi. This was essentially the effect of Pepsi's branding message of life being full of excitement and enjoyment.

This research may suggest that if you feel you share values with something, then your perception of it is likely to be different than someone who does not. This can be a flaw when you consider that something such as fizzy pop in fact has no such intrinsic values. Biases like these are important to consider when you are trying to uncover personal meaning.

This tool can help

It's often hard to take time out of our busy lives to reflect and consider what is it that we really want, who we want to be and what is really important to us. This tool is about how to identify your personal meaning and highlights the importance of being aware of your core values and personal preferences. Knowledge of these core concepts can help you to understand what you want from your work and how to go about getting it.

● PERSONAL MEANING DECONSTRUCTED

There is so much going on around us and we are subject to so many external influences that, sometimes, it can be hard to identify your own direction or core identity in life. Understanding who you are and what really matters to you is about identifying your 'personal meaning'. At first, this might seem a little obscure – a bit like trying to describe 'the real me' in one easy sentence!

However, its relevance in the workplace is that whomever you believe yourself to be and what your personal ethics are is likely to determine the way in which you behave and interact with others. It also has a bearing, therefore, on your own alignment or otherwise with the job you do and the overall goals and objectives of the organisation which employs you.

People often begin their job motivated and invest considerable effort in it but, for some, this dwindles. So, ask yourself why you do what you do. Whatever your personal circumstances, it's always useful to reflect on what's really important to you, who you are and what you want. We can't promise too much, but as a starting point this tool is designed to give you a little more personal insight about what matters most to you.

● THE FOUR UNDERLYING CONCEPTS

Personal meaning constitutes these four, separate concepts:

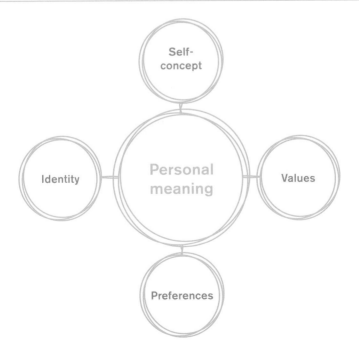

● THE CONCEPTS DEFINED

These descriptions of its four elements will help to explain 'personal meaning':

Self-Concept[2] – A person's knowledge and understanding of his or her self

Who we believe we are and how we would describe ourselves is our 'self-concept'. It's what makes us decide where we 'fit' amongst, and compared to, others and provides us with consistent physical, psychological and social attributes. These could include all kinds of characteristics from being of sound mind to having particular beliefs. It provides an overall consistency of personality and behaviour as we tend to behave in ways in keeping with our self-concept. Many of our successes and failures are closely related to the ways in which we've learned to view ourselves and our relationships with others.

Identity[2] – The distinct personality of an individual

It's the individual characteristics, deriving from our personalities, by which we're recognised or known. They can include things such as family continuity and other affiliations or associations with others, or a recognisable separateness from others.

Values[3] – Personal ethics or beliefs in which we have an emotional investment

Our values influence the choices we make; they're subjective and vary across people and cultures, resulting from circumstances, experiences and observations – and can change over time. For example, our choice of a new car may be influenced by values to which we subscribe, including status, price and family situation.

Preferences[3] – This is what may influence your choices, motivations and behaviour

For example, if you prefer dealing with figures to reading or writing, you may look for a job in finance rather than publishing.

These concepts guide us every day but it's our values and preferences which decide our behaviour and actions. They're what we'll focus on now, to try to answer this question:

'Why do I do this job?'

● 'WHY DO I DO THIS JOB?'

Step 1 – Record your values

Use the following table to capture your core values – those which matter to you most. These could include traditional, core values such as a sense of fairness, hard work and respect for others, or whatever you choose. To help you decide, ask yourself the following questions:

- What are your most important beliefs?
- What is really important for you?
- Which principles guide your day-to-day behaviour?
- What issues would you fight most strongly for?

My Core Values

Step 2 – Identify your preferences

Having noted your core values, another major influence on your behaviour will be your personality or behaviour 'preferences'. You may already know what these are, or have completed a test to establish them, such as the Myers Briggs Type Indicator.[4] However it's still useful to summarise your preferences before completing 'Step 3'. Typical preferences can include being optimistic, trusting others and being busy with a variety of things to do. Answering the following questions will help you with this:

- What do you particularly enjoy?
- What motivates you?
- What makes you particularly happy?
- What are your particular strengths in the way you relate to others?
- What do you most enjoy doing at work?

My Preferences

Step 3 – Complete the checklist

Once you have established your values and preferences, you've essentially started to consider what drives you and what you may enjoy doing. Use the checklist below to identify those aspects that are important to you, to identify the type of role that may suit you. If you strongly agree with a statement, give it a double tick and if you partially agree with a statement give it a single tick. If you don't agree with one at all, leave it blank:

Checklist		
Dimension	Statement	Tick
Reward or recognition	1. I enjoy being rewarded for my efforts.	
	2. I have a need to be recognised for my work.	
	3. I consider my work to be of some benefit.	
	4. I am motivated by financial reward.	
Role content	5. I have chosen a career in a specific sector or industry.	
	6. It's important that I enjoy the type of work I do.	
	7. I am motivated by the type of work I do.	
	8. I use knowledge I have gained to help me in my role.	
Social aspects	9. I work to provide for my family.	
	10. I enjoy working with others as part of a team.	
	11. I feel that the work I do benefits the wider community in some respect.	
	12. I believe in giving something back to society and I do this through my work.	
Personal development	13. Learning and developing is important for me.	
	14. I want to develop myself in my current role.	
	15. I have a career path and am constantly moving towards an overall aim or a set of objectives.	
	16. I learn from experience in order to help me in the future.	

Step 4 – Establish your core dimension(s)

Using the checklist, identify which dimensions you have ticked the most. These are likely to be core 'drivers' that will shape your approach to work and your typical behaviour. The table below provides some points to consider for each dimension:

Dimension	Considerations
Reward or recognition	• You're likely to be motivated to have a secure financial income or by receiving 'just' reward or recognition for your work. • You are someone who will value a reward-based system and feel that people should be recognised for the effort they make. • Consider whether the environment in which you currently work caters for your need to be rewarded or recognised.
Role content	• You're likely to be specific about the type of role which you take on. • You would probably prefer it if your job related to your experience. • Consider whether the environment in which you currently work caters for your need to use your knowledge in your role and to enjoy the type of work that you do.
Social aspects	• You're likely to be motivated to do a job that has some benefits for the wider community. • You may enjoy the social side of the working environment and are motivated to work with other people. • Consider whether the environment in which you currently work caters for your need to see the social side of your job and the wider benefits to the community.
Personal development	• You're motivated by learning and development and it's probably important for you to be continuously developing in your role. • You may benefit from working in an environment where experience, mistakes and successes are learned from. You may enjoy a role where there is a structured career path. • Consider whether the environment in which you currently work caters for your need to grow and develop and meets your ambitions and goals.

You should now have a better idea of your values and preferences and what you really want from your working environment.

Example

Consider the following example of someone completing steps 1-4:

Values identified: Hard work, integrity, work ethic, family.

Preferences identified: Works well with others, likes to be busy, gets the job completed, complies with rules, will take calculated risks.

Dimensions identified: reward or recognition and social aspects.

This person's values seem to be linked to their preferences and dimensions. Two themes seem to emerge: importance of a social aspect and the value of hard work. However this does require further exploration.

They may want to consider the following points:

- Are they motivated by receiving reward or recognition?

- They seem to like working with others and have identified social aspects as a 'driver' for them. Are these linked together? If so how?

- Which are their strongest values, preferences and motivators?

- They say that they may take calculated risks. How would they balance this with their intention to behave with integrity?

Like the person in this example, you may appear to have consistent threads linking your values with your motivations, or they may be less clear. Don't worry if your values, preferences and motivators don't seem to link up; this tool is about raising your awareness of what you want in order to reappraise the work that you do now, or would like to do.

HINTS AND TIPS

The following hints and tips can be applied to many core value combinations:

1. Once you have identified the values that are most important to you, consider whether they're catered for in your current role or type of work. What does this mean in terms of what you are doing now and what you really want to achieve?

2. Consider how your values and preferences guide your behaviour and actions.
   a) Draw a vertical line down the middle of an A4 sheet.
   b) On the left side write the most important preferences you have identified. Spread them out evenly.
   c) On the right hand side of the page, think about the main behaviours that you demonstrate.
   d) Try to note down 10-15 behaviours; for example, project management, line manager to four people. Number each behaviour.
   e) Below each dimension, note down the behaviours (by number) that these guide in your work. (You may have some you can't categorise.)

   This should help you recognise how you behave according to your personal values and preferences in your job. Think about the things that you'd like to be doing, what you could do more or less of, in order to work according to your values and preferences. The closer the match between your work and your values the easier it's likely to be for you to carry out your day-to-day activities.

3. Consider the values which you have ticked and especially those which you have double ticked. How much does your current job allow you to live your values and do the kind of things you prefer? You may want to refer to your original job description, if you have one, to help remind you what your job's really all about!

   Think about how your values and preferences impact others. Consider whether others know what your core values and preferences are.

4. Talk to your team members and arrange for some time, for example on an 'away day' or during a team meeting, where you can discuss your values and preferences and those of your team. You may want to get your team to complete the 'Why do I do this job?' exercise, too!

● NEXT STEPS

This tool is designed to focus your thoughts on what you really value and how this affects your approach to your work and what you want out of life. Consider the following suggestions for practical next steps:

Discuss your values and preferences

Consider discussing these findings with someone you trust, such as a line manager, coach, mentor, colleague or even friends and family to gain different perspectives and to consider your way forward.

Write a development plan

If you don't already have a personal development plan and/or career plan it is well worth investing the time to put one or both of these together. Ensure that you give yourself clear objectives and tangible actions that will help you to progress and make a real improvement. This will help you identify your goals and aspirations as well as how far you have gone to meet them.

Complete a value/preference personality questionnaire

It can be useful to gather more information to increase your levels of self-awareness and provide you with more information about your values and preferences. Take a personality test to measure your values and preferences in more detail. Some tests focused on values and preferences include:

- Hogan Motivation, Values and Preferences Inventory (MVPI™)
- Saville Wave Questionnaire™
- Myers Briggs Type Indicators Questionnaire (MBTI™)

Some of these tests are widely available, and others need to be administered by a qualified professional, such as a Pearn Kandola psychologist.

Also, if you found this tool useful, then a good next step to take would be to go through the iLEAD™ tool 'How to capitalise on self-awareness'. This will inform you not only how to put your newfound awareness of your own personal meanings to good use, but those of your colleagues as well.

We're all unique

Everybody has different values and preferences and it is up to you to decide how best to behave according to your personal profile. Good luck!

● FURTHER INFORMATION

If you found this tool useful then you are likely to find the following tools both insightful and relevant:

- How to identify personal learning styles
- How to focus on the bigger picture
- How to make ethical decisions
- How to get the most out of yourself.

● REFERENCES

1   Allen, M., Gupta, R. & Monnier, A. (2008). The Interactive Effect of Cultural Symbols and Human Values on Taste Evaluation. **Journal of Consumer Research**, 35, 294-308.

2   Huynh, Q. L., & Banaji, M. R. (2012). **Handbook of Self and Identity** 2nd ed.

3   Roberts, L. M., Cha, S. E., Hewlin, P. F., & Settles, I. H. (2012). Bringing the inside out: Enhancing authenticity and positive identity in organizations. **Exploring Positive Identities and Organizations**, 149.

4   Myers, I. B. (1962). **The Myers-Briggs Type Indicator**. Consulting Psychologists Press.

HOW TO BE AN EFFECTIVE ROLE MODEL

Understand which behaviours are important for you and your business, as well as gaining practical advice on how to role model effectively.

● ISN'T IT INTERESTING?

Too much to drink?

Excessive alcohol use in US colleges has been called a 'recalcitrant problem'. One of the ways that has been researched as a possible weapon to combat the problem is the use of role modelling. Students who were unfamiliar with heavy drinking were far more likely to be influenced by role models who drank heavily and were more likely to engage in the same behaviour than those who were already familiar. The conclusions taken were that role models who did not drink excessively could have a positive impact by making contact with new students who were not familiar with the drinking culture of a new university.

Do violent films affect behaviour?

Researchers in the 1960s[1] studied the effect of punishment on participant behaviours and learning. They paired participants with a stooge (a fake participant) for a 'learning task'. Before the start of the task the participants watched either a violent or non-violent film with a starring antagonist/protagnoist. Then, as part of the learning task, the participants were told to give the stooge an electric shock whenever they made a mistake. The participants were able to control and change the level of shock for each trial. The result of the experiment was that those who observed the violent film would shock in higher intensities than those who watched the non-violent movie.

While the claim that violent films can increase violence in individuals in the real world is highly contested, evidence like this shows how role models can affect our behaviour. The effect has been found to be particularly strong on children where there are high levels of ambiguity and uncertainty.

This tool can help

We can pick up behaviours from all kinds of role models and this does not just happen in childhood, as many think. This tool is about how to be an effective role model and aims to help you to understand which behaviours are important for you and your business, as well as providing practical advice for how to role model effectively.

 # WHAT MAKES A ROLE MODEL?

Who is your role model?

Who have been the most significant role models in your life? Why are they role models for you? Are they all the same? Are they all different? It is worth taking a moment to consider these questions as it is often these people who will consciously, or subconsciously, guide some of your actions and behaviours.

What is a role model?

You have probably been told by your team or manager that you should be a 'positive role model' or that 'you need to display role model behaviour'. But what do people mean when they talk about role models?

Maybe the easiest way to approach this is to consider some of the popular role models of our own and previous times, such as John F Kennedy, Nelson Mandela, Oprah Winfrey, Richard Branson and others. These people possess very different qualities yet all can be labelled role models. For example, you could say that Nelson Mandela was inspirational because he stood for what he believed in and followed a difficult course to achieve an end. You could say that Richard Branson has built a business empire from very little through sheer hard work, dedication and passion.

What is it about these people that makes them role models? Social psychology research about leaders reveals them to be above averagely intelligent,[2] talkative,[3] considerate (people focused) and more able to define objectives and organise work (task focused).[4] Think back to your own role models and whether they had all or some of these qualities.

Why is being a role model important?

Most people have aspirations or people they admire. From an early age, we learn through watching others and copying their behaviour (with both positive and adverse consequences!). Role models can influence people's thinking and behaviour in both personal and working environments, often motivating them to take on challenges and achieve for themselves.

According to theory,[5] watching the behaviour of another person can produce a 'cognitive representation' in the observer, whose actual behaviour may be influenced accordingly. This is a model or 'ideal' that we build in our mind and refer to when we are faced with taking action and decisions.

So, it's important that a role model's behaviour exemplifies the values to which they subscribe. In a corporate environment, there is obvious purpose and benefit in setting examples of conduct and performance for employees to emulate.

Aspiring role models can discover more about 'living out values' in the tool 'How to identify your personal meaning'.

For now, consider the following questions:

- Who are my role models?
- Why are they important?
- Who can I be a role model for?
- How do I currently 'stack up?'
- What should I do?

Below we outline a model of the common attributes for being an effective role model against which you can assess yourself.

● ROLE MODEL CORE FEATURES

The core features of being an effective role model are outlined below:

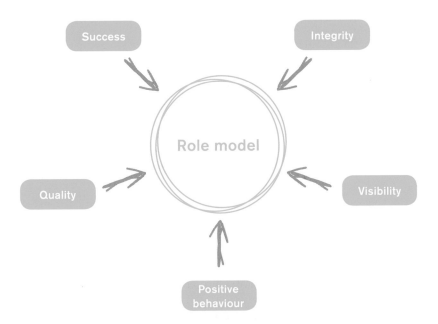

● CORE FEATURES BREAKDOWN

Success

When you think of people you admire, most of them have either achieved something you value, e.g. a lifestyle, money, status, or have a capability such as caring for colleagues or being considerate. People often gauge how effective a role model is by the level of success they have achieved. It is therefore important to understand what success means and what target to aim for. Whatever the end goal, it is important to consider the impact that this will have on others. Every person who is, or aspires to be, a role model should consider whether 'good' is enough.

Integrity

This element is all about ensuring that you live out certain values. This may be about adhering to company values or behaving in line with certain personal values. An example of a common value that both organisations and individuals hold is hard work. Putting in hard work leads to success. For a role model to be effective they have to be seen to be putting in the effort in order to reap the rewards.

Quality

People often admire things that are of a high level of quality, such as a top-of-the-range car or a piece of craftsmanship. This focus on quality is itself considered of high value. In organisations, working to, and insisting on, high levels of quality tends to produce outstanding results. For example, if you are leading a new project you may want to ensure that people clearly understand what level of quality you expect. You could point to similar, previously undertaken tasks or projects in order to benchmark the quality levels you require. It is worth showing people how you personally will aim to reach these high standards. This enables others to see the standards that you expect and how you will adhere to these quality levels. It is then up to you to live out this plan and produce work of an extremely high quality.

Positive behaviour

There are many different types of role models, but all will display some form of positive behaviour. This can cover a range of different actions or activities. The important aspect is that these behaviours are linked with some form of success or value set. That is, the behaviour leads to a successful result or the approach itself sets a good example for others, regardless of the outcome.

Take the scenario of negotiating a business deal. Examples of positive behaviours in this situation could include:

- Sticking to a game plan for negotiating a win-win outcome
- Being honest about what can and can't be compromised
- Facilitating meetings to involve all parties
- Communicating the progress and outcomes with all stakeholders.

Visibility

Part of role modelling effectively is ensuring that people can see what actions and behaviour is being undertaken. Maintaining a visible profile is important to ensure that the approach can be seen by others in order for them to learn from it. This is not just about status for the sake of maintaining a certain profile but can be used to help others understand what good behaviour is, or how to conduct themselves. In this way people can better understand what success looks like and how it can be achieved.

The following pages outline two practical tools to help you to be an effective role model:

- Common misconceptions
- Role model attributes Self-analysis.

● COMMON MISCONCEPTIONS

There are a number of common myths about how a role model should look or behave – some of which are examined below:

Myth	Reality Check
You need to be 'charismatic' to be an effective role model	● Charismatic people are often seen as being outgoing, sociable and 'lighting up a room'. They may be people who can inspire others or have a passion for what they do. ● These attributes may be useful and there are, and have been, many charismatic leaders and role models. However, it really does depend on what you are trying to embody. If you are showing good practice around a procedure do you need to be charismatic? No, and this is a common myth that can be put aside. ● You do not NEED to be charismatic to be an effective role model.
You have to be seriously successful to be considered a role model	● Success is often one of the key elements of a role model. The most crucial aspect is to understand what success actually means in each situation and why this is particularly important. ● Often it is not the outcome but the approach that is the important part of the action or behaviour. Of course, success can be a good benchmark of whether behaviour works or not, but role models do not have to be extremely rich or have high status or power. ● You do not HAVE to be seriously successful to be considered a role model.
I couldn't be a role model	● A lot of people may not consider themselves to be the right 'material' to be role models. This may link to the 'charisma myth'. However, there is no reason why you cannot be considered a role model. Look at what you are doing, how you are doing it and what you have achieved. ● When you start to take a look at yourself you should be able to find some aspects that you find important and that you embody and that other people would look up to. ● You CAN be a role model.
Role models are good at everything	● Many people make the mistake of looking at role models and taking their good qualities out of proportion and projecting this onto their whole being. ● Role models often show bad behaviours as well as good ones. It is often a particular aspect that you may admire in someone. Be careful not to project this attribute to an overall view of someone without good evidence. ● Role models are not perfect; they too have their faults. Often you can have more than one role model and concentrate on different qualities for each person. ● You do NOT have to be good at everything to be a role model.

● ROLE MODEL ATTRIBUTES SELF-ANALYSIS

To find out what type of role model you are use the following tool to highlight your preferred approach.

Step 1: Complete the self-analysis questionnaire

Complete the self-analysis questionnaire using the key below:

Key:

1. I always do this   2. I often do this   3. I sometimes do this   4. I rarely do this   5. I never do this

	Role model attributes self-analysis	1	2	3	4	5
1.	I produce high quality work.					
2.	I have a clear set of values that I conduct my behaviour around.					
3.	I judge myself and others on the results that are achieved.					
4.	I behave in line with the company values.					
5.	I keep a visible profile so that people can see what I am doing well.					
6.	I set challenging targets for myself.					
7.	I carry out my tasks in an open and honest fashion.					
8.	I work hard to ensure that I achieve success.					
9.	I demonstrate the correct behaviours at work for the tasks that I have to do.					
10.	I let people know about my successes and how they were achieved.					
11.	I do my best to hit or exceed aims and objectives.					
12.	I behave fairly towards the people I work with.					
13.	I try to achieve the best outcome possible and direct my focus on the results.					
14.	I adapt my behaviour to be as effective as possible in any situation.					
15.	Whenever possible, I let people see what I am doing in order to learn from my approach.					
16.	I encourage those around me to achieve high standards.					
17.	I do not cut corners for short-term wins over longer-term success.					
18.	My success is based on achieving specific aims and objectives.					
19.	I behave fairly towards the people I work with.					
20.	I keep myself in the limelight in order to ensure that my work and successes are noticed.					

Step 2: Scoring the self-analysis questionnaire

Use the following process to score your results. Look at each category and add up the corresponding ratings:

Area	Items to Add	Total
Quality	1, 6, 11, 16	
Integrity	2, 7, 12, 17	
Success	3, 8, 13, 18	
Positive behaviour	4, 9, 14, 19	
Visibility	5, 10, 15, 20	

Step 3: Consider your strengths and development needs

Look up the one or two categories where you have the lowest score to find out your main approach to role modelling:

Area	Your Approach to Role Modelling	Considerations
Quality	You focus your approach on ensuring that you hit the highest possible levels. This approach often links to integrity – if you have high standards as a core value then you are likely to try and meet these goals.	Consider what success looks like for you and how you set about showing the positive behaviours which demonstrate to others exactly how you reach those peaks. Think as well about how visible you are in showing how you work to your high standards and therefore how others can learn from your approach.
Integrity	Your approach centres on ensuring that you behave according to a set of personal/ organisational values. This will often link in with positive behaviours that you want to display and may be linked to having high standards.	Consider whether you are showing others the attitude and behaviours with which you are trying to conduct yourself. Do people know how your approach will help you, and them, to succeed?
Success	Success and reward is a key driver for you and you are likely to judge your effectiveness on your output. You are likely to have a focus on achieving the end goal and direct your actions and behaviours accordingly.	Consider how much you take your approach into account. Other people may be more concerned about the approach you take to achieve success as well as the outcome itself, i.e. are you being ethical? Do you consider the people you work with? Also, how much do you publicise your success?

Area	Your Approach to Role Modelling	Considerations
Positive behaviour	You are focused on ensuring that you carry out tasks and activities using good behaviours. This may vary from task to task but you will always try to ensure that you do things in the best possible way to set an example for those around you.	Consider how much of an example you are setting to others and whether the behaviours you are using are the most appropriate for each situation. Also bear in mind how effective these are in achieving the end result and reaching high quality levels.
Integrity	Your main aim as a role model is to maintain a high profile in order that others can see what you do and adapt their behaviour accordingly. Your role could be to portray a certain approach or to behave in a particular manner.	Consider what you are making visible to others. Are you showing people that you adhere to a set of clear values? What are the positive behaviours that you are portraying? How do you show success in a way that will inspire others?

Now consider how you can capitalise on your preferred approach to be the most effective role model possible and how you can take the other aspects into account, or develop these areas.

● NEXT STEPS

Now that you have considered the factors involved in being an effective role model and have some practical tools to consider, it is worth thinking about what to do next. Here are a number of suggestions to maintain momentum:

Gather feedback on existing performance

You may find it useful to benchmark your current performance by asking for formal or informal feedback.

Seek out role models

Consider who the role models are in your life and your organisation. Once you have identified the people and their various aspects that you admire or would like to emulate, think about what it is particularly that you admire about them or their approach. You may then want to think about how you compare. This may seem daunting if you feel that there is a big gap but this is the starting point for you to develop a plan to improve.

Write a development plan

Use the tool in this document to highlight your role model approach. Once you have established your preferences you could put together a focused development plan to improve your effectiveness as a role model for others.

Look for opportunities to practise

Think about the opportunities that you have in your current work, or beyond, where you can practise role modelling good behaviour or improving your profile.

● FURTHER INFORMATION

If you found this tool useful then you are likely to find the following tools both insightful and relevant:

- How to identify your personal meaning
- How to identify personal learning styles
- How to get the most out of yourself
- How to make ethical decisions.

● REFERENCES

1   Walters R. & Doan, H. (1962). Reported by Lamont, N. (1962). Report on the O.P.A. 1962 Annual Meeting. The Canadian Psychologist. Apr 3a(2) 67-70.

2   Mann, R. (1959). A review of the relationship between personality and performance in small groups. Journal of Personality and Social Psychology, 42, 260-272.

3   Mullen, B., Salas, E. & Driskell, J. (1989). Salience, motivation, and artefact as contributions to the relation between participation rate and leadership. Journal of Experimental Social Psychology, 25, 545-559.

4   Stodgill, R. (1974). Handbook of Leadership. New York: Free Press.

5   Bandura, A. (1977). Social Learning Theory. Englewood Cliffs, NJ: Prentice Hall.

HOW TO IDENTIFY PERSONAL LEARNING STYLES

Understand the characteristics underlying different learning styles and find out how to identify your own learning style. Explore different learning styles to find out how others learn.

● ISN'T IT INTERESTING?

Do as I say, not as I do…..?

Learning through imitation

One way we learn is through imitation. When we watch other people role modelling behaviour, we learn how to do things and also recognise what is and isn't acceptable behaviour. This can be particularly seen in children as they develop; many parents will have examples of situations where their children have picked up both desirable and undesirable habits by imitating them. However, this is not just a childhood phenomenon but a way of learning that we use throughout our lifetime.

How do you learn best?

In 1983, Dr. Howard Gardner[1] developed the theory of multiple intelligences. This suggests that there are different types of intelligence and our learning style will depend on the type of intelligence we have. Likewise, knowledge of these intelligence types will help us to understand how we can begin to identify the learning styles of those around us.

The different types of intelligence identified were:

- Linguistic intelligence (words)
- Logical–mathematical intelligence (numbers or logic)
- Spatial intelligence (pictures)
- Musical intelligence (music)
- Body-kinesthetic intelligence (physical experience)
- Interpersonal intelligence (social experience).

So when you have had difficulty grasping or understanding a topic, consider the different ways in which the messages can be communicated to tap into your preferred learning method.

This tool can help

Knowledge of our personal learning styles is important to ensure we tap into the learning styles that we can use most effectively. This tool is about how to identify personal learning styles and will help you to understand the characteristics underlying different learning styles and how to identify your own learning style. Different learning styles will be explored to help you consider how others learn.

● LEARNING STYLES ARE IMPORTANT

Why is it important to consider your learning style?

How easily do you learn new techniques or processes, assimilate information and generally adapt in a continually evolving business environment? Have you noticed that some members of your team are more motivated or better adapted to learn than others? If you're planning a developmental activity for yourself or them, understanding that we all have preferred (and therefore more effective) methods of learning could save time and money, or make the difference between partial and complete success.

Kolb's experiential learning theory model[2]

This well known theory suggests that the way an individual learns is linked to his or her preferences or choices, and that it is a continual, cyclical process of experience, reflection, thought and finally action. Action involves experimentation or testing, which leads to a new, different experience, and so the cycle begins again.

During the observations and comparisons which led him to this theory, Kolb identified four different ways of learning – or 'personal learning styles':

Diverging

A mixture of concrete experience and reflective observation.
This is a preference for watching rather than doing. People who learn this way tend to have an 'open minded' attitude and work best in groups, or situations where different perspectives are available to compare or amalgamate with their own interpretation, to reach an understanding or solution.

Assimilating

A mixture of abstract conceptualisation and reflective observation.
A preference for a concise, logical approach with good clear explanation. People who learn in an 'assimilative' way are able to comprehend a wide-ranging variety of information and organise it clearly and logically. They may appreciate the logic and theory of a proposal, rather than its practical application.

Converging

A mixture of abstract conceptualisation and active experimentation.
People with a converging style of learning like to experiment with new ideas which they can then use practically – they tend to prefer technical tasks.

Accommodating

A mixture of concrete experience and active experimentation.
An approach which uses given data, or other people's analysis, to work out a practical solution. Such people like challenges and new experiences, often acting on 'gut instinct' rather than logical analysis. They may prefer to work with others to complete tasks.

As with any behavioural model, these are guides, not rules. Nevertheless, most people demonstrate one or other of these tendencies and don't alternate between them easily – learning more effectively when the method is oriented towards their preferred style.

People who have a clear learning style preference will tend to learn more effectively if learning is orientated according to their preference.

Next, we'll outline personality characteristics which may determine learning styles.

● PERSONALITY PROFILE – THE BIG FIVE

There has been much research, over many years, into what constitutes 'personality'. Much of it, however, refers to what is known as the 'Big Five' characteristics, around which all aspects of personality centre. Many studies over the last few decades have shown the relevance of this form of profile characterisation to job performance.[3] The 'Big Five' personality traits are also the basis of the most widely used personality questionnaires.

Conscientiousness
A tendency to show self-discipline, act dutifully, and aim for achievement; planned rather than spontaneous behaviour.

Openness to experience
An appreciation for art, emotion, adventure, unusual ideas, imagination, curiosity, and variety of experience.

Extroversion
Energy, positive emotions, self-confidence, and the tendency to seek stimulation and the company of others.

Agreeableness
A tendency to be compassionate and cooperative rather than suspicious and antagonistic towards others.

Neuroticism
A tendency to experience unpleasant emotions easily, such as anger, anxiety, depression or vulnerability; sometimes called emotional instability.

The Big Five

It's easier to remember the 'Big Five' using the acronym OCEAN. They're as follows:

O Openness to experience

Openness to Experience describes a dimension of personality that distinguishes imaginative, creative people from down-to-earth, conventional people. 'Open' people tend to be intellectually curious, appreciative of culture and aware of their feelings. They therefore tend to hold unconventional and individualistic beliefs, although their actions may be conforming. People with low scores for 'openness to experience' tend to have narrow, commonplace interests. They prefer the plain, straightforward and obvious to what is complex, ambiguous or subtle. They prefer the familiar to the novel, and are resistant to change.

C Conscientiousness

This is about regulating and directing our impulses. Conscientious individuals tend to avoid trouble and achieve success through purposeful planning and persistence. They're regarded by others as intelligent and reliable, but can, if they veer towards perfectionism or 'workaholism', be thought stuffy or boring. Unconscientious people may be criticised as unreliable, unambitious and unconventional, but they'll experience many short-lived pleasures and are often considered by others to be colourful, spontaneous and fun to be with.

E Extroversion

Extroverts engage strongly with the external world. They're energised by others, often have a positive outlook and tend to be enthusiastic, action-oriented individuals. In groups they like to talk and assert themselves. The opposite of extroversion is introversion, and those with this tendency are likely to be quiet, low-key, deliberate, and less dependent on external stimuli – they gain their energy from within. Their lack of social involvement should not be interpreted as shyness or depression; the introvert simply needs less stimulation than an extrovert and more time alone.

A Agreeableness

Agreeable individuals have an optimistic view of others and value getting along with them. They're therefore considerate, friendly, generous, helpful and willing to compromise. They tend to believe that people are basically honest, decent and trustworthy. Disagreeable individuals place their own interests above those of others, are generally unconcerned with their fellows' wellbeing and less likely to extend themselves on another's behalf. Scepticism about others' motives can make them suspicious, unfriendly or uncooperative.

N Neuroticism

Neuroticism is an emotionally negative tendency. Emotional response to events will be more intense than others' and more likely to be negatively interpreted. Minor frustrations may be exaggerated. Conversely, individuals who score low in Neuroticism tend to be calm and less negative or emotionally reactive. This doesn't, however, mean they could be described as particularly 'positive', which is a characteristic of extroversion.

Understanding your personality profile will help you to determine your preferred learning styles, in line with Kolb's experiential learning theory

On the following pages we've provided a self-analysis questionnaire which, while not validated, will indicate your strongest tendencies. This will help define which learning style you prefer.

● PERSONALITY – LEARNING STYLES INVENTORY[3]

This questionnaire designed by Kolb et al. based on the aforementioned 'experiential learning model' will help you to determine the most effective methods of learning for you, according to your personality.

Step 1: Complete the self-analysis questionnaire

Complete the questionnaire by indicating the extent to which you agree with each statement, using the key below:

Key:

1. Strongly disagree 2. Disagree 3. Sometimes like me 4. Agree. 5. Strongly agree

	Role Model Attributes Self-Analysis	1	2	3	4	5
1.	I have lots of ideas.					
2.	I tend to take a back seat in meetings and discussions.					
3.	I'm always prepared.					
4.	I'm uncomfortable expressing my feelings and other personal things or creative thinking.					
5.	I can start conversations with anyone.					
6.	I am keen to try out new ideas to see if they work.					
7.	I'll take time out of my work for others.					
8.	I love to solve a crisis.					
9.	I worry about things.					
10.	I have excellent ideas.					
11.	I look at things from all angles and consider implications.					
12.	I get things done right away.					
13.	I don't let my feelings influence my decisions.					
14.	I like being the centre of attention.					
15.	I get frustrated and impatient with longwinded or open-ended discussions.					
16.	I can feel others' emotions.					
17.	I get fully involved in new experiences.					
18.	My mood changes a lot.					
19.	I have a vivid imagination.					
20.	I mull things over before reaching conclusions.					
21.	I follow schedules a lot.					
22.	I rigorously question assumptions and conclusions.					

	Role Model Attributes Self-Analysis	1	2	3	4	5
23.	I am the life and soul of the party.					
24.	I like solving practical problems and making decisions.					
25.	I am sympathetic to others' needs and feelings.					
26.	I will try anything at least once.					
27.	I often feel down about things.					
28.	I spend time reflecting on things.					
29.	I prefer to stand back and observe.					
30.	I pay close attention to details.					
31.	I can link different facts to form coherent theories.					
32.	I feel comfortable around people.					
33.	I use my experience to find solutions.					
34.	I make people feel at ease.					
35.	I am open minded and enthusiastic.					
36.	I get irritated or upset easily.					
37.	I am quick to understand things.					
38.	I gather lots of information before solving problems.					
39.	I ensure high quality levels in my work, and that of others.					
40.	I think problems through logically, step by step.					
41.	I talk to people in all kinds of different social situations.					
42.	I work to the principle that the end often justifies the means.					
43.	I am interested in people.					
44.	I get bored by detail.					
45.	I get stressed out easily.					

Step 2: Scoring the self-analysis questionnaire

Now you've completed the questionnaire, calculate your score for each of the 9 areas (that is, the 4 learning styles we described at the beginning plus the 5 personality characteristics of the 'Big Five'), in the table below. To do this you need to add your scores for each set of five questions relating to each area. For example:

Openness – questions 1, 10, 19, 28 and 37 make up this area. To calculate your score for Openness, look at the box you ticked for Q1 (strongly agree to strongly disagree) and note down your score for that question (this will be between 1 and 5 and is shown on the heading for the table). Now do this for questions 10, 19, 28 and 37 and add them together. Write the number in the total column of the table below.

Repeat this process for each area, adding up your scores for the corresponding questions shown in the table.

Area	Questions to Add	Total
Openness	1, 10, 19, 28, 37	
Diverging	2, 11, 20, 29, 38	
Conscientiousness	3, 12, 21, 30, 39	
Assimilating	4, 13, 22, 31, 40	
Extroversion	5, 14, 23, 32, 41	
Converging	6, 15, 24, 33, 42	
Agreeableness	7, 16, 25, 34, 43	
Accommodating	8, 17, 26, 35, 44	
Neuroticism	9, 18, 27, 36, 45	

Step 3: Identify your learning styles

Your main personality preference (the Big Five factor you would most strongly associate with) will determine your combination of preferred learning styles. Below, we have matched each personality preference with the most likely combinations.

Using the scores you entered into the table above, add each 'area combination' and write your total in the box for each in the Personality – Learning Styles Matrix below. For example, if you score 10 on Openness and 12 on Diverging then enter 22 in the grid, in the 'Dreamer' box.

Personality – Learning styles matrix:

Personality Preferences	Learning Style Combination			
	Diverging	Assimilating	Converging	Accommodating
Openness to Experience	Dreamer	Connector	Inventor	Puppy
Conscientiousness	Analyst	List Maker	Piston	Monitor
Extroversion	Socialite	Facilitator	Coordinator	Explorer
Agreeableness	Sponge	Fluffy Robot	Family	Volunteer
Neuroticism	Jelly	Lawyer	Rebel	Yo-Yo

So, for example, if you clearly demonstrate extrovert characteristics; that is, you enjoy being with people, are energetic, outgoing and open to challenges or new experiences, your learning styles combination is likely to be 'EXPLORER'.

Step 4: Prioritise your learning style combinations

This stage will list your learning styles in order of preference. The higher the combined score, the more likely it is to be your favourite and most effective style.

Use the following table to prioritise your learning styles. Enter the title of the highest scoring combination, followed by its score, for example 'Sponge' 25.

Priority	Learning Style Combinations	Total
1.		
2.		
3.		
4.		
5.		
6.		
7.		
8.		

The table on the following page provides a summary of each learning style combination. Using this information consider your priority learning styles. The following questions may help you to clarify your thoughts:

- Which style do you tend to use the most?
- Which style for you is most effective?
- Does your style vary across different situations?
- How can you capitalise on your preferred learning style(s) to ensure you learn in the best way for you?

● LEARNING STYLES COMBINATIONS[3]

Learning Style Combination	Summary
Dreamer	Spends time reflecting and considering information. Needs plenty of time and space to digest it, which may produce more thought and ideas. May seem 'in a world of their own'.
Analyst	Learns by reflecting on and 'chewing over' information. Needs time to think about what is being learned and its implications. May not seem interested in learning at times, because can appear distant or uninvolved.
Socialite	Will listen and begin learning to an extent but will be more interested in others involved – or what else might be going on – than in the learning itself. May find it difficult to concentrate at times
Sponge	Soaks up information. Can digest a lot of data. May not challenge statements or decisions made – even if disagrees or contrary evidence is apparent.
Jelly	Registers information but then tends to worry, either about the information itself, or about own ability to use it correctly or appropriately.
Connector	Synthesises new information with own experiences and the 'wider picture'. May lose attention to detail if learning is not closely managed or monitored.
List maker	Organises information and plans schedules in order to assimilate information. Very organised and focused. May have a tendency to be overly prescriptive or inflexible.
Facilitator	Opens up discussions, challenges assumptions and involves others. Will aim to involve others in the learning in order to test it and gather evidence to establish facts or views.
Fluffy robot	Wants to make logical challenges, but is keen not to upset others. Will challenge in a very 'nice' way! May be gauging other people's views and feelings about the information.
Lawyer	Logical and factual approach. Considers the evidence for and against the learning but forms own opinion. Will happily test this out on others to check concerns. This person's tendency to challenge could be interpreted by others as 'just being objectionable for the sake of it'.
Inventor	Comes up with new ideas or different angles and considers how they would work in practice. Will try out theories or assumptions for the same reasons.
Piston	A doer. Will progress learning by considering and applying the practical aspects or enabling others to. May become overly focused on the practical elements of learning to the detriment of the theory.
Coordinator	Works with others to show practical aspect of learning. May find it difficult to learn alone, preferring to do so with others to establish its relevance or applicability. Danger of coercing others to learn when they don't want to!
Family	Tries to learn with others. Learns best when practising with others who also want to do so. Works to help self and others to learn. Could slow the learning process by taking time to ensure everyone is happy with it.
Rebel	Learns in own way. May feel constrained and frustrated by impractical or slow learning and will often take own, different course of action in order to learn. May upset, annoy or frustrate trainers.
Puppy	Open to new experiences and keen to try out new techniques. Could 'drain' others as it's not always apparent this individual has absorbed information before moving on to the next thing!
Monitor	Open minded and willing to take on challenges, albeit reasonably cautious. This is a 'look before you leap' mentality.

Learning Style Combination	Summary
Explorer	Curious and willing to learn but needs to involve others in the process and tell them 'all about it' – may side-track or dominate group learning.
Volunteer	Will assist others to learn and share experiences. Concern for others is helpful but may at times hinder own learning.
Yo-Yo	Changeable approach to learning. Enthusiastic one minute, uninterested the next! Very dependent on personal interest in subject matter and mood.

The following section outlines the next steps for you to consider now that you have identified your preferred learning styles.

● NEXT STEPS

You should now have an understanding of the variety of learning methods preferred by different personalities and you should also have identified your own. So what next? Here are a few suggestions for maintaining momentum (although they are by no means exhaustive):

Test yourself

You may have an opportunity to do this formally – but why not find an area of interest to test your learning style. You could try different approaches to find out which are most effective.

Look for opportunities to practise different learning styles

You may have identified learning styles you've never used or even considered before. Try them anyway; you may find them surprisingly effective. Opportunities might include:

- Formal courses
- Structured activities
- On-the-job activities
- Off-the-job activities
- Open learning
- Books, reading
- Videos/DVDs.

Write a development plan

Information about learning styles can be used to make your own and your team's development plans more appropriate and therefore more effective.

● FURTHER INFORMATION

If you found this tool useful then you are likely to find the following tools both insightful and relevant:

- How to identify your personal meaning
- How to develop others
- How to get the most out of yourself.

● REFERENCES

1 Gardner, H. (1983). **Frames of Mind: The Theory of Multiple Intelligences.** Basic Books.

2 Kolb, D. (1981) **Learning styles and disciplinary differences.** in A. Chickering (ed.) The Modern American College, San Francisco: Jossey-Bass.

3 Barrick, M. R., & Mount, M. K. (2006). The big five personality dimensions and job performance: a meta-analysis. **Personnel psychology,** 44(1), 1-26.

4 Kolb, D. A. (1999). **Learning style inventory.** McBer and Company.

HOW TO DEVELOP OTHERS

Increase your awareness of the key steps necessary to develop others, the potential resources to use, and different formats that can be used for development planning.

● ISN'T IT INTERESTING?

From tiny acorns mighty oaks do grow...

Developing others

Helping others to grow and develop is vital in the talent management strategy of any organisation. We know that providing development goals that are stretching but attainable is the first step, but people don't learn and develop in isolation – others play an important part in the process too. 'Scaffolding', i.e. providing support at the outset but then gradually reducing it as someone becomes more proficient, is a technique that can help to increase competence and development.[1] A key part of the scaffolding process is giving feedback, the importance of which was highlighted in the study below.

The importance of feedback

Using a natural setting to investigate the importance of feedback, psychologists set up an experiment in a high school in the Basque region of France.[2] For a year, they provided regular updates to the schoolchildren about where they ranked compared to the class average and how far away they were from it. As a result, the class exam average went up by 5% overall; however, after the year was over, the improvement from the experimental year disappeared.

It is possible to draw two important conclusions from this data. Firstly, that regular objective feedback can obviously be an important motivator, whether it is positive (being higher than the average), or negative (being lower than the average). However, it is just as important to maintain this feedback, and also for it to be capitalised on, otherwise the positive benefits can be lost over time. This applies in the workplace as well as the classroom, and this tool will help you to deliver regular, effective feedback in order to develop others.

This tool can help

Feedback can have an impact regardless of whether it is positive or negative – the aim is to make it constructive and meaningful. There are many factors besides feedback that you can use to successfully develop others and help them to succeed at varying levels. This tool is about how to develop others and will help you to increase your awareness of the key steps necessary to develop others, the potential resources to use, and different formats that can be used for development planning.

● INTRODUCTION TO DEVELOPING OTHERS

What do you think it's all about, this business of managing other people? Not so long ago, the stereotypical manager was a slightly removed figure, but 'in charge' – clocking us in and out. It was a matter of ensuring achievement of specific functions and processes, by those assigned to carry them out. And still, this must be a manager's fundamental purpose.

But there's a whole lot more to it now. Not only do businesses need to constantly adapt and change to keep pace with technological advances and changing working methods, they also need to keep up with the need to develop employees' skills in tandem. However, employee development is not only about what will benefit an enterprise. Employees themselves expect it and will often walk if it's not made available because, according to research, it motivates people as much if not more than money. Without opportunities to grow, people leave their jobs. And they blame their managers.

Developing others is therefore one of the most crucial elements of your role as a manager.

Unfortunately, the responsibility of developing other people is often thrust upon managers who, while extremely competent in their technical areas of expertise, are less skilled in knowing how to help others develop. These people can be labelled 'bad bosses' and are often pointed to as the reason for individuals leaving their organisation, with the most common specific reason being their 'bad boss' did not provide opportunity for career growth and development.[3]

'People don't leave jobs, they just leave bad bosses'

This tool provides straightforward insight into the key steps required for managers to effectively develop their employees. It also provides hints and tips for managers on key aspects of the process.

THE DEVELOPMENT MODEL

Eleven key steps have been identified for developing others. These are described in the following DEVELOPMENT model:

D Data collection

E Exchange of views

V Vision of the future

E Environmental awareness

L Learning styles consideration

O Options for development

P Planning action

M Maintaining momentum

E Evaluating progress

N New directions

T Taking stock

THE DEVELOPMENT MODEL – STEP BY STEP

Data collection

This is the first thing to do. You need to start by gathering information about the role and the person involved. That means identifying gaps between actual and required performance, as well as assessing future requirements of both person and role. This information will provide the basis for a discussion between the two of you, and agreement about how to proceed.

Exchange of views

The point of this is to decide where development is needed and the result should be a mutually agreed list. The process should involve both sharing your views gained from data collection and exploring the views of the individual in relation to their development.

Vision of the future

This would be explored in the 'exchange of views' discussion, but we've separated it to highlight the important difference between identifying an individual's current proficiency or otherwise, and describing how this might evolve (and what the individual would like to achieve) in future.

Environmental awareness

Once you have identified which areas need to be developed, you will need to work with the individual to decide what to do. Your plan will need to take into account how much time they have available, whether any expense will be involved and, if so, getting this appropriately sanctioned, beforehand.

Learning styles consideration

This requires finding out how the individual prefers to learn. This is more important than it might sound – people have different, preferred ways of assimilating information and getting this wrong could waste time and money. There are four learning styles[4] which suit the majority of people:

1. **Activists:** people who enjoy new experiences and learn best when thrown in at the deep end!
2. **Reflectors:** people who prefer to listen, review and analyse before making decisions.
3. **Pragmatists:** those who learn best by putting ideas into practice.
4. **Theorists:** people who synthesise ideas and information through exploration.

If you want to investigate different methods of learning further, have a look at another of our tools called 'How to identify personal learning styles'.

● OPTIONS FOR DEVELOPMENT

The individual may have his or her own ideas about how to achieve the objectives agreed in your earlier discussion with them (such as external or online training). Or you may be able to make suggestions about strategies which have previously worked for others. You will also have more knowledge about what's going on elsewhere in the workplace which might be useful (opportunities to shadow others, perhaps, or to attend meetings and presentations).

Planning action

It's all very well thinking up a list of great ideas but, unless they're written down, they're unlikely to happen! Ask the individual to write down what their goals are, together with their own ideas about how they might be achieved.

A study showed that the 3% of a surveyed group of graduates from Yale University who had written goals in 1953 had accumulated more wealth than the other 97% altogether when asked about their financial position 20 years later.[5]

Maintaining momentum

By this stage, the individual should have a written action plan which, if implemented, will result in their measurable development. The very fact that it's all written down will help them focus! However, for many, this isn't enough. People often start with great intentions – then get distracted and before they know it, their brilliant plan's just another file on the shelf, next to all the others. (As manager, it's your job to encourage as well as direct, so, if you find this is a common problem amongst your team, there's another tool to help you, called 'How to maintain momentum'). Ways to keep people focused include linking the stages of their development to their annual performance objectives, arranging regular review meetings, encouraging the individual to allocate regular times in their diary to focus on development activities, and pointing out that development is a gradual, continual process rather than an overnight revolution. In other words, it's better to do a little at a time than a week of feverish activity followed by months of inertia.

Evaluating progress

You need to evaluate progress regularly. This might be observation or feedback from others. When you talk to the individual about your findings, make sure you give praise as well as indicating what needs attention, if necessary.

New directions

People and organisations change. Often, what was once useful becomes inappropriate or redundant. If it becomes apparent that amendments need to be made to an individual's development programme, be flexible.

Keep the development plan alive, and there's more chance that the individual will develop.

Taking stock

It's vital to take stock of both the individual's achievements and your own performance in facilitating development. For the individual, this is about the extent to which objectives were met – taking into account any amendments or other things beyond their control, along the way! Where goals have been achieved, give praise and recognition. If not, a discussion should take place about what needs to change (in either the person or the plan). Encourage individuals to tell you whether the way you've handled things was helpful or otherwise.

For you as a developer of people, it is important that you continuously learn from your experiences. Encourage the individuals that you are developing to give you feedback on the extent to which you have been helpful. What are the things you did well and what things could you have done better? Use this information to produce your own development objectives in relation to how you could become even better at developing others.

● SOURCES OF DATA

Here's our checklist of things to find out about an individual and their role, before embarking on a development plan:

The Role Requirements (Present and Future)

The job description.

The 'person specification'.

Their annual objectives.

Their development plan.

Organisation's competency framework.

Benchmarking data; that is, information about what others in the same role are currently doing.

Information about competitors; that is, information about what competitors are currently doing.

Business plans and strategic documents; that is, information about skills required to meet future business needs.

Information about advances in areas of expertise.

Individual Performance

Feedback from them.

Feedback from their staff.

Feedback from peers.

Feedback from customers.

Your own observations.

Performance data, for example, were sales targets met?

Reports from any development activities, for example, development centres.

● AGREEING DEVELOPMENT GOALS

Development goals will emerge from both organisational (current and future) and individual needs. Your role is to ensure that, as far as possible, both are met. If development goals are weighted too much in favour of organisational needs, the individual may feel less motivated.

Try to achieve a reasonable balance and agree what the goals are, with the individual and senior members of the organisation, as appropriate...

You can do this through open and constructive discussion, and we've got a suggestion about how to do this next.

● PROCESS FOR AGREEING DEVELOPMENT GOALS

1. Agree an agenda for the meeting.
2. If necessary, clarify everyone's purpose in the meeting and whether the discussion needs to be confidential.
3. Ask questions to encourage the individual to offer their own view of their strengths and development needs.
4. Actively listen (that means acknowledge what they say, or just nod, to demonstrate you are giving your attention) and agree or challenge as appropriate.
5. Give your own views of the individual's strengths and development needs, using information you've collected, and give examples.
6. If necessary, clarify what the organisation requires of them and any timescales given. This may be simply that you want them to be in line with what is expected of someone in their role or it may focus on new skills that will stretch them to take on new responsibilities.
7. Ask questions to encourage the individual to describe their aspirations and motives.
8. Where possible, make links between these and the business's requirements.
9. Agree a manageable number of development goals – too many will overwhelm and de-motivate the individual.

● OPTIONS FOR DEVELOPMENT

Here's a framework of some different methods of development, the suitability of which you can assess according to environmental influences and personal, preferred methods of learning. For example, to achieve the development goal of speaking conversational French, you could consider an open learning package, an evening class or a secondment to a French office.

Development Goal:		
Development Option	Suitable for the Environment? Yes/No	Suitable for the Learning style? Yes/No
Training course Specific example: _____		
Open learning with DVDs, CD, computer, etc. Specific example: _____		
On-the-job activity Specific example: _____		
'One-off' work assignment/project Specific example: _____		
Secondment Specific example: _____		
Reading (books, articles, manuals, etc.) Specific example: _____		
Shadowing/observing others Specific example: _____		
Practising skills, for example, role play Specific example: _____		
Coaching Specific example: _____		
Mentoring Specific example: _____		
Networking/sharing experiences Specific example: _____		
Conferences/seminars Specific example: _____		
Development centre Specific example: _____		
Outward bound/team building events Specific example: _____		

Development action planning

It's vital that a plan for someone's development is written, because it clearly explains what is intended to all involved, and achieves greater commitment. Here are the kinds of headings you might use:

For each DEVELOPMENT GOAL you should document:

Actions:
The various actions needed to achieve the development goal.

Timescales:
A clear timescale for achieving the development actions.

Potential barriers:
Any barriers that prevent the development goals being achieved; for example, time, budget constraints.

Overcoming barriers:
Actions to address potential barriers.

Resources:
Any resources; for example, time, money, people and equipment needed to achieve the goals.

Development Goal:	1	2
Actions		
Timescales		
Barriers		
Overcoming barriers		
Resources		

Development Goal:	3	4
Actions		
Timescales		
Barriers		
Overcoming barriers		
Resources		

Learn from past experience

Using the DEVELOPMENT model, identify things you didn't do in the past. Ensure these are included next time when developing others.

● NEXT STEPS

Think about the following when you're next planning someone's development:

Review your past performance

How well have you developed your staff to date? What aspects of the DEVELOPMENT model did you adhere to? Did you collect appropriate information? Did you give the individual concerned a chance to make suggestions? Did you make sure they wrote down what they planned to do?

Get feedback from the people you manage

Ask the people you manage to give you feedback about the extent to which their development goals were agreed. Did you achieve a healthy balance between the business's needs and those of the individual? Did you agree an agenda? Did you ask questions to encourage them to talk? Did you challenge their assumptions? Did you give your own views? Did you discuss their aspirations? Did you link their aspirations to business objectives?

Gather information

Gather information to help you develop people more effectively. This might include information about the role requirements of the people you manage, the extent to which they're meeting them, future business requirements, up and coming development opportunities and a budget, if appropriate.

● FURTHER INFORMATION

If you found this tool useful, then you are likely to find the following tools both insightful and relevant:

- How to maintain momentum
- How to motivate others
- How to influence others
- How to manage difficult conversations
- How to create team identity
- How to gain buy-in and commitment
- How to support and challenge in tandem
- How to identify personal learning styles
- How to formulate action plans
- How to delegate.

● REFERENCES

1   Ross, L., Lepper, M. & Hubbard, M. (1975). Perseverance in self-perception and social perception: Biased attributional processes in the debriefing paradigm, **Journal of Personality and Social Psychology**, 32, 880-892.

2   Ribes, E., & Rodriguez, M. E. (2011). Correspondence between instructions, performance, and self-descriptions in a conditional discrimination task: The effects of feedback and type of matching response. **The Psychological Record**, 51(2), 9.

3   Liz Simpson (2001). Divorcing the Boss, **Personnel Today Magazine.**

4   Honey, P. and Mumford, A. (1986). **A Manual of Learning Styles** Peter Honey, Maidenhead.

5   Harrold, F. (2002). **The 10 minute life coach** Hodder and Stoughton.